On JORDAN'S STORMY BANKS

Other Books by H. Beecher Hicks Jr.

Preaching through a Storm
Correspondence with a Cripple from Tarsus
My Soul's Been Anchored

LEADING YOUR CONGREGATION

through the

WILDERNESS *of* CHANGE

On
JORDAN'S
STORMY BANKS

H. BEECHER HICKS JR.

ZONDERVAN™

GRAND RAPIDS, MICHIGAN 49530 USA

On Jordan's Stormy Banks
Copyright © 2004 by Kerygma Associates, Inc.

Requests for information should be addressed to:
Zondervan, *Grand Rapids, Michigan 49530*

Library of Congress Cataloging-in-Publication Data

Hicks, H. Beecher
    On Jordan's stormy banks : leading your congregation through the wilderness
of change / H. Beecher Hicks Jr.—1st ed.
       p. cm.
    Includes bibliographical references.
    ISBN 0-310-24774-8
    1. African American clergy—Biography.   2. African Americans—Religion.
3. Hicks, H. Beecher.   I. Title.
BR563.N4545 2004
253—dc22

                                    2004005091

Interior design by Michelle Espinoza

Printed in the United States of America

---

04 05 06 07 08 09 10 /❖ DC/ 10 9 8 7 6 5 4 3 2 1

For
Austynn Lené Hicks
Ashley René Hicks
Henry Beecher Hicks IV
Harrison Patton Hicks
our progeny and our hope
and
the Metropolitan Family
for your partnership on the journey

*Destiny is no matter of chance. It is a matter of choice:
It is not a thing to be waited for, it is a thing to be achieved.*

Gary Hamel and C. K. Prahalad
Competing for the Future

—ଚ୨ ଚ୨—

*Then a cloud covered the tent of the congregation, and the
glory of the LORD filled the tabernacle.*

Exodus 40:34

CONTENTS

FOREWORD

Seldom are we given the opportunity to peer into the heart and soul of a person who has been given an awesome assignment from God. Yet in *On Jordan's Stormy Banks,* we are given a glimpse into the inner thoughts and struggles of a true prophet of the kingdom of God. Dr. H. Beecher Hicks goes with his work where few are willing to go. He takes us into the soul of the preacher and causes us to see that there are many moves on the chessboard before one can say, "Checkmate."

When we accept the call of God first to preach God's Word and then to pastor God's people, we have no idea where that will take us. Preaching is the vehicle we use to communicate the message, but pastoring is the art of leadership, enabling people to get to the places God has purposed for them. Dr. Hicks makes it clear that the pastor's burden is heard in his preaching and the preacher's struggle is felt in pastoring. However, he affirms that the Word of God is the answer and hope for the church and its individual members. He is not one who would replace preaching with fancy serendipities; he confidently affirms that it is through preaching that vision is seen, understood, and embraced.

I hope that all who read this work will begin to sense what it takes to craft a sermon. I hope that you will see that only as the preacher bares his soul, with its fears and hopes, can a sermon emerge. A sermon is not three points and a poem; nor is it just a verse-by-verse discussion; it is a window into the soul of the preacher who sits with God. These messages allow us to hear the conversation between the preacher and God as God gives direction for building His house.

Dr. Hicks uses the sermons in this book to guide the people of the Metropolitan Church into their new destiny. "How shall they hear without a preacher?" is the word he utters. God gave him the sermons to help the church see the vision. Sermons must speak to vision, and vision must birth sermons. The preacher who would see vision come to reality must use the gift of the sermon to slowly walk the people to their promised land. Dr. Hicks begins this journey with Israel unaware of all that will be unfolding and marches us with the command, "And let them make me a sanctuary. . . ." Vision is not caught quickly; it must be nursed, and it must be protected.

Without a doubt, the new Metropolitan Church will be an awesome structure. I was in the worship service on the Sunday the architect was given his charge. That charge reflected weeks and months of vision casting, powerful preaching, and the faithful witness of a people with heritage and history. The new facility will be a marvel to many, but the members of the church, and those who read this work, will understand the journey undertaken by a pastor and people who "stood on Jordan's stormy banks and cast a wistful eye to Canaan's fair and bountiful land."

Dr. Walter Scott Thomas
Pastor, New Psalmist Baptist Church
Baltimore, Maryland

PREFACE

These are the writings of a parish priest—nothing more, nothing less. God ordained that the task of preaching be performed by the parish priest. The day-to-day work of proclaiming the gospel is not the work of prophets, who typically are briefly heard and then seen no more. Rather, it is the work of the parish priest who, with faltering footsteps, stammering tongue, and a sense of his or her own frailty, seeks to be faithful to a task that is simultaneously awesome and awful. We who struggle with the task of being both priest and preacher do so under an awesome imperative to speak words we often do not fully understand to those who very often do not wish to hear.

By and large, preaching is a pastoral calling. Preaching is not the work of academicians, though it must be informed by the contribution of those who are a part of academia. Nor is preaching exclusively the work of theological professors who struggle in their own God-directed journey and who have the frightful and thankless task of training pastors for this work. Preaching is the weekly task of those who are engaged in an arduous journey with the Eternal—a continuous life struggle to find words to say that come from a Source outside ourselves. Preaching is born in the soul of one who has, in the words of the late Peter Marshall, received a divine "tap on the shoulder." It is because of that "tap" that a preacher embarks on an eternal, God-directed journey.

On Jordan's Stormy Banks reflects a portion of my pastoral and spiritual journey over more than twenty-five years as senior minister of the Metropolitan Baptist Church congregation. In many ways, it is a journey I did not seek; neither is it a journey from which I can escape. The writings contained herein are technically Sunday morning sermons with all the excessive verbiage and archaic language that typify the preaching moment. Sermons, as Dr. Gardner Taylor has said, are indeed "clumsy tools."

In looking back over my preaching of the last few years, however, I was surprised to see that over and over God had been guiding me to the Moses narratives that speak of how God prepares a people and a leader to move. This is not to suggest that my sermonic offerings were without prior thought; rather, it is to suggest that I had hoped to use a biblical text that would be far easier to interpret to the contemporary mind. Part of the difficulty with these sermons, which are taken from the book of Exodus, has been to demonstrate how ancient texts are relevant to the postmodern mind. Sermons on the construction of the tabernacle of ancient Israel do not evoke great excitement, because at first glance they do not seem to provide help with the issues of daily living, nor do they appear to be germane to the human condition. It seems irrelevant in this age of terrorism and war to be preaching about the building of an ancient tabernacle in an effort to help the congregation understand what God requires of them to build their own.

Yet the preacher's task remains. He or she must take what God is doing and what God is saying, even when it appears to be irrelevant, and open it up widely enough that it becomes prophetic—a *rhema,* living word of God. These sermons reflect the effort of one parish priest to achieve that awesome task. More than that, these sermons are pieces of worn and frayed fabric that speak of an ongoing process that has shaped the faith and vision of a pastor and his people. They prove again the theory that every challenge and crisis faced by the church can only be adequately and meaningfully addressed through the faithful proclamation of the gospel. They also underscore the belief that no matter how outdated the Bible may seem or how irrelevant the process of preaching may appear, God still uses this medium to give the guidance and vision needed in especially perilous times. In every situation, no matter how deep our distress and confusion, God's Word is still a lamp to our feet and a light to our path.

These sermons also raise critical questions about the life of the church, the meaning of ministry, and the relationship between church and community. They provide insight into my own calling, particularly as it relates to my determination to shape the life of a congregation in accordance with the vision God has given me. Without question, I myself struggle to understand the meaning of that vision and the way it must be cast for it to be realized. Therefore, these writings also contain an honest assessment of my own struggle for clarity and purpose. The printed versions of these sermons cannot capture the spiritual moments in which they were delivered. Sermons are prepared not for the eye but for the ear; they are heard best in the context of the "call and response" motif that is typical of the African American church. In these instances it is the author's hope that the reader will be charitable when faced with the peculiarities of this preaching and writing style.

This is not an easy story to tell. It does not have a "happily ever after" ending. In fact, I do not know how the story will end. At this writing, we are still laboring over many of the issues raised in these pages. We are still endeavoring as a congregation not only to complete the journey, but also to make sense of the journey.

The fact that we cannot yet see what the end will be may cause some to question the timing of this volume. I must admit that I considered reserving this volume for the time when we will have achieved our desired outcome, when the new tabernacle for the Metropolitan congregation has been built, when Metropolitan has emerged with a renewed focus on ministry and our viability as an institution within the community has been restored. I considered holding out until "happily ever after" arrived. To do so, however, would have defeated my purpose.

My purpose in telling this story is to help other pastors and church leaders who are facing similar challenges in finding meaning for the traditional institutional church. This work will reveal the frustrations and the faith, the anxiety and the assurance of one parish priest seeking to be faithful to his calling. This account seeks to illuminate the role of vision in the local church, which is informed by the complex relationship between the church and the secular culture in which the church operates, suggesting methods that allow the parish priest to speak authentically to both.

I would like to thank Katherine V. Stanley of Atlanta, Georgia, owner of Scribe Writing and Editorial Service and associate editor of *Black Issues Book Review* magazine, for her invaluable assistance with this book.

THE SETTING

From its inception, the Christian church has not been without its share of challenges. Indeed, most of the apostle Paul's writings are dedicated to dealing with conflicts and challenges within the churches of his day. The Revelation of John contains critiques of seven churches of that day. No church, in Paul's day or in ours, can escape either conflict or challenge. Moreover, the pastor can never escape the unenviable task of dealing with these conflicts and challenges as they arise. A pastor's ability to do so effectively requires a rare blend of wisdom and courage.

Like most churches, Metropolitan has faced its share of challenges. Our most recent challenge occurred as a result of the changing complexion, if you will, of the urban Washington community in which we are located. Born during the last days of slavery, this church has historically been a part of an urban environment. More particularly, its ministries have always been targeted to the surrounding community. It has been and remains a beacon of hope within a community originally known as Hell's Bottom. The church quickly grew to a size larger than its facility and, while parking was always a problem, the problem became more urgent as the surrounding community was increasingly populated by people who had no connection with the African American church and did not value Metropolitan's contributions to the Shaw community.

In what seemed to be a determined effort to change the shape and texture of the community, our new neighbors challenged the church's right to use the Garrison Elementary School's yard for parking. Metropolitan was the subject of a local news report that portrayed us as heartless and selfish for denying children the right to play baseball on the field. In an effort to prevent the school's right to lease the property to the church and to force our departure from the field, the community sued the school board for relief.

It needs to be said that the challenge we faced was not simply a parking problem. What was stake here was a redefinition of community: Was there still a role for an urban megachurch in it? The challenge for the church was to engage in meaningful conversation with its new neighbors. The challenge for the changing community was to live in peace with a large institution that had established its presence there more than a century ago.

I knew this was a fight we would never win. And given the impact of our having a facility that was too small for the growth of our ministry, I knew that it was a fight we had no stake in winning. My desire was to bring closure to the conflict in a way that allowed Metropolitan to maintain her historical significance and integrity. Yet I was angered by what I perceived as deliberate efforts by the new residents to publicly destroy our previously amicable relationship with the Garrison School. My ultimate goal was to move the church toward a new definition of ministry in the new millennium. This conflict with the community was getting in the way. The inaugural sermon in this book, "How to Handle Life's Trials," was delivered as a means of providing a spiritual context for a worldly dilemma.

INTRODUCTION

Visioning in the Modern Church Context

I will stand upon my watch, and set me upon the tower, and will watch to see what he will say unto me, and what I shall answer when I am reproved. And the LORD answered me, and said, Write the vision, and make it plain upon tables, that he may run that readeth it. For the vision is yet for an appointed time, but at the end it shall speak, and not lie: though it tarry, wait for it; because it will surely come, it will not tarry.

Habakkuk 2:1–3

The notion of vision is important to any thoughtful analysis of ministry in the local church. But what is vision? Is it a mere prediction of a more desirable future when compared to a current condition? Is vision merely setting priorities? Is it a vehicle for communicating to others what we desire to do? Does vision in the church context encompass different dynamics from the vision that Bill Gates has for Microsoft, that Bernie Ebbers had for WorldCom or that Jack Welch had for General Electric? How different is vision for the secular and sacred worlds? How can one know and verify that a vision is eternal (God-directed) as opposed to temporal (human-directed)? How does a pastor come to understand a congregation's vision? Conversely, how can a congregation come to accept and appreciate the integrity and honesty of the pastor's vision?

Within the African American church community, congregations have traditionally looked to the pastor for vision and direction. By and large, the dynamics of African American congregations have changed because of higher educational levels and an increased knowledge of business, administration, and finance. African American congregations have also changed because members have higher levels of education than previous generations and there is an increasingly sophisticated and high number of scholarly learners and student-disciples who have the ability to examine and evaluate what the church is and is not saying. As a result, the pastor is no longer considered the exclusive vision caster. Instead, the pastor is viewed by some as the "front person" who gives voice to the plans and strategies that have been designed in a far savvier church boardroom. The days of "whatever the pastor says goes" are, for the most part, a thing of the past in the African American church. Thus the notion of vision has become far more complicated in terms of the way vision is cast and the way vision is received. The pastor is the initial receptor of the vision. Nevertheless, it remains the responsibility of the pastor to speak the word of that vision with such clarity that its authenticity is never in doubt.

The modern congregation has changed in another significant way. Unlike the church of my rearing, where a congregation could be relied on to be faithful in attendance, disciplined in its approach to church management, and devoted to matters of theology and doctrine, regrettably today's congregations have in many instances become audiences or spiritualized assemblies. Even the casual observer can detect that the commitment to the church as an institution is lukewarm at best. Because the pool of committed church attendees has shrunk so drastically, the task of identifying and nurturing strong lay leadership has become increasingly difficult. Moreover, as churches grow, developing congregations into a church family is more challenging. We preach, therefore, not to congregations, but to crowds and audiences who come for the purpose of being entertained while having their immediate personal and spiritual needs addressed. A broader vision for the church in terms of its mission and witness appears to be the last thing on most churchgoers' minds.

Nevertheless, a clear vision statement is necessary because it helps both pastor and church understand where the ministry is going, how it is going to get there, and what the desired outcomes and expectations are once it has arrived. Vision is vital for ministry. Without vision, people cannot see or grasp their direction.

The matter of vision becomes even more complex when the pastor discovers that what he or she sees is entirely different from what the people see. The inescapable and relentless task of the watchperson-priest is to labor with worn-out tools until those who hear are also able to see. Remember that Moses on Mount Sinai had to "turn aside and see" what God was attempting to communicate (Exod. 3:3). Therefore, vision must not only be cast, vision must be taught repeatedly. A vision once spoken is twice forgotten, but a vision that is spoken with regularity and precision (and, as with Moses, dramatically!) makes its way to the head and subsequently to the heart.

Within most churches, and surely within the traditional African American church, the sermon is the primary vehicle for communication available to the minister. The preaching moment is the time when the priest-watchperson is able to share his or her message with a large number of people in one place. The use of sermons as an instrument to cast vision may raise significant questions in the minds of some church attendees. Is vision casting a legitimate use of the sermon? Should the pastor use the advantage of his pulpit to "lobby" the congregation for what may appear to be his own "pet project"? If not through the sermon, what other vehicle is available to the preacher for appropriate and effective communication? These questions deserve honest answers.

Some people may argue that they do not come to church to hear the pastor talk about his or her next great venture. Rather, they come to hear "the Word," to be inspired and encouraged. They do not come to be regaled regarding a building that will require them to increase their giving. On more than one occasion, I have heard someone say, "I did not come here for that!"

This criticism may have some legitimacy, because it is possible for a priest-watchperson to use the sermon as a tool to manipulate the congregation. After all, the preacher has a "captive audience" on Sunday morning and can take advantage of such a lofty place of power. Whether this manipulation occurs has much to do with the relationship the pastor has with the congregation. If in the relationship between pastor and congregation the pastor holds a substantial amount of power, the sermon may indeed be used in a manipulative manner. If, on the other hand, an appropriate balance of power exists between pastor and congregation, the sermon may be used appropriately to mold thought, modify behavior, or speak a word from the Lord. In that sense, the sermon is not manipulative. Rather, it is the essence of what authentic preaching is all about. Properly conceived, the sermon becomes the word of God when it addresses the human predicament with power and redemptive grace. Indeed, it is through the strange grace of preaching that the Word of God transfigures and transforms people as well as institutions.

In my view, the sermon is an appropriate vehicle for vision casting that is unique to the church. It certainly is not a tool that may be used in the corporate, economic, or political worlds. But without the sermon as a vehicle for communicating vision in the church, leaders would be at a loss for relating what God seeks to share with God's people.

Nevertheless, while the sermon is a vital tool for vision casting, the methods and means of casting one's vision must not be limited to the sermon alone. A wise priest-watchperson will engage numerous strategies for spreading the visionary message. In our highly technological world, ways to reach the people of God with the Word of God seem to increase almost daily. If the sermon is the only tool used, the congregation may be engaged for a moment, but what was said will not register in the deeper places of the heart where commitment, dedication, and loyalty to vision are developed.

The task of all preaching is to declare the Word of God with such clarity and power that those who hear experience it and accept it as authentic. When the Word is perceived as God's Word, and there is an anointing and power upon that Word, not only is the sermon a fit vehicle, but the people will expect the sermon to be used to cast visions. Most will come to the worship hour not seeking a word from the deacon or trustee boards, but seeking the living Word of God. The prophet Jeremiah was asked, "Is there any word from the LORD?" (Jer. 37:17). If there is, the priest-prophet-watchperson must tell it, publish it, make it plain, and write the vision with such clarity that "he may run that readeth it" (Hab. 2:2).

PREACHING
the VISION

PART I

A Prelude to Preaching

If Moses, or any other man, had been commissioned by God to design a portable building for the purpose for which the tabernacle was to be used during Israel's wilderness journeys, it could well have proved a "mission impossible"; therefore, so that nothing would be imperfect about it, God designed it himself.

Cecil Jennings,
The Glory of the Tabernacle

Good morning, my prophet:

Your task, should you choose to accept it, is to guide my people to a land I have chosen and prepared for them. They will not wish to travel. They far prefer their bland diet and their guaranteed employment. They will not see what you see. They will not hear your words. They will not accept your leadership. You will experience much pain in the process. This may seem an impossible assignment. Do not forget, I specialize in the impossible. Of course, should you, Miriam, Joshua, or Caleb follow my leading, I will not fail you or forsake you. Just speak my words . . . no matter what! I will always be with you.

Love, God

There are moments in every pastor's life when God sends a divine e-mail and it seems that the pastor is the only one who received it. When such moments arrive, the pastor is in the unenviable position of relaying a message to the people, who view it as irrelevant at best. It often falls on blind eyes and deaf ears. In such moments, making a sacrificial commitment to the vision and using the preached word to impart the vision are essential. Like Ezekiel, a pastor must assume the role of priest-watchperson if he or she is to effectively communicate that vision to the people and colabor with them in embracing the vision, assuring its fulfillment. If a pastor does not prove to be up for the task, any attempt to bring the vision to the people and the people to the vision will prove futile. This Prelude to Preaching admonishes and instructs pastors who would be visionaries.

> But if the watchman see the sword come, and blow not the trumpet, and the people be not warned; if the sword come, and take any person from among them, he is taken away in his iniquity; but his blood will I require at the watchman's hand. So thou, O son of man, I have set thee a watchman unto the house of Israel; therefore thou shalt hear the word at my mouth, and warn them from me. (Ezek. 33:6–7)

When a corporation seeks to cast a vision, it uses the expertise of public relations specialists who design and test strategies that will assure buy-in from the audience it desires to influence. Similarly, when a retailer wants to increase its profits and positively impact the bottom line for its investors, it hires an advertising firm to spend millions of dollars on television, radio, print media, and other forms of advertising to cast a vision that creates an inextricable identity for the product it seeks to sell. In the spiritual realm, when God casts a vision, God does so through the preacher and preaching.

Strange that God would choose to use a preacher—a mere mortal, made of frail and sinful stuff—to declare the word of redemption and salvation. God, it would appear, does have some television time on cable networks managed by a wide assortment of televangelists who send a broad and generic message. Yet God still requires a human vessel to proclaim and interpret a specific vision for a specific people at a specific time for a specific purpose. God has no public relations specialists or media experts to cast the vision for him. God must resort, therefore, to methods that are as old as the Bible itself.

In today's world, it often seems that God's time-honored method of casting vision, by the preacher through the preached word, has been rendered irrelevant. The church, in an age of rising secularity, appears to be caught in a web of increasing irrelevance. Within the African American community in particular, the church is no longer the center of communal life. The church appears to have lost its moral high ground. The church is no longer the locale of social protest. In this world, the church and its spokespersons are rarely consulted on issues of ethical importance the way they once were.

Also readily apparent is the impression that the church is no longer the center of our social life. In times past, the church provided the outlet for our leisure activity and entertainment. Today other options vie for our leisure hours. The church is left wondering where the people went. Many megachurches boast of drawing astounding crowds on a regular basis, but the average church in America—black or white—has no "Standing Room Only" sign in its foyer.

Pity the preacher who appears to be doomed to preach from an archaic book that seems to have little or no relevance for a cyberspace generation. Pity the preacher whose only musical frame of reference is an anthem or hymn no one cares to sing because "hip-hop" and "rap" have captured our musical ears. Pity the preacher who must stand to proclaim a word he says comes from God to people who are not really interested in that word or that God. As far as this generation is concerned, God is alarmingly aloof, silent, and insignificant.

The signs of the time in this culture appear to indicate that no one has heard from or is listening to God. As a result, the preacher is always on precarious terrain whenever he or she dares to claim to have received a vision from God.

As I look around my office, I see volumes of manuscripts, books, and the like that represent my life and the lives of countless other preachers spent casting God's vision through the spoken word. I cannot help but think, therefore, that if preaching has become irrelevant, then so have I—so have we. To the contrary: I believe now, as I have for the past four decades, that my assignment is to cast God's vision for the world, for my community, and for the little flock for which Christ has made me responsible.

Despite my passion for and experience in vision casting, I must honestly grapple with the question of how anyone can truly know whether he or she authentically speaks God's vision. Deep questions arise in my own spirit: What is God's vision anyhow? Why is God's vision seemingly always shrouded in mystery and enigma? Why can't God speak plainly and in my own native tongue? How can I trust the vision to be God's when the vessel through which the vision is given is often weak and wicked? Has God's vision changed over the years, or is it the same vision that is in the Bible we continue to use? Is God still casting the same vision He always has cast? If God is in a continual process of making "all things new," how is that newness detected? How can one determine if the "new thing" God is doing can withstand the critique of this present age?

For some of us, while the urgency to preach remains the same, the context in which that preaching is carried out has changed dramatically. Even so, I am still convinced that God has deliberately chosen a peculiar vessel—a mere parish priest—to preach the gospel, to declare His Word, and to cast the vision for what God seeks to achieve in this world. This divine selection notwithstanding, the preacher who stands before the congregation on a Sunday morning declaring a vision from God must be conscious that he or she will come under awful scrutiny.

Called to Preach

An expression from the African American church experience speaks about "the call." Every Sunday in the Mount Olivet Church in Columbus, Ohio, where I grew up, the worship service began with "devotions" led by the deacons. In more contemporary black churches, it is called "praise service." But when I was growing up, the deacons held devotions! Without fail, at the conclusion of these devotions someone would rise with this word of testimony: "And for those of you who know the worth of prayer, I want you to pray for me. I want you to pray my strenck (strength) in the Lord, and pray that I be the one he be calling for in these last and evil days. . . . For these is perilous times!"

Truer words have never been spoken. For if one is to declare a word that is authentically the word and vision of God, one must be certain that he or she is "the one He be calling for." One must understand that God has choices in whom He calls. By every available measure of biblical interpretation, it is clear that God has complete ownership of the calling process. Stated more bluntly, everybody who claims to have been called has not been called by God.

Some years ago, our church experienced a season during which a dramatic number of members acknowledged "the call" to ministry. One of the deacons who discussed the phenomenon with me offered this analysis: "Pastor, I don't know why all these folks are talking about being called. If it's so, it appears that God has Metropolitan's phone book, and He's calling everybody!" I do not propose to question another's call, but I do know that "the call" is a very serious matter, especially in light of the fact that "these is perilous times."

The Ezekiel Paradigm

Part of understanding how God's visioning process works is to understand that God calls the preacher to a particular task in perilous times. The prophet-preacher Ezekiel is instructive for us here.

Ezekiel lived during a time of captivity and slavery, a time when Judah had suffered political destruction. Judah's captivity, which began in 606 BC, lasted until 536 BC, a total of seventy years. The nation's life was marked by diminished political power and deepening religious apostasy and idolatry. The nation was spiritually and morally weak in every sense of the word. Judah was so weak that it had become a cemetery of the slain, and the bones of the dead were "very dry" (Ezek. 37:2).

Scholars tell us that Ezekiel was in training for the priesthood during the Babylonian exile, but God had something else in mind for him. During Israel's darkest hour, God called Ezekiel to be a prophet. At a time when the nation all around him was in the throes of defeat, Ezekiel's preaching assignment was to warn Israel that Jerusalem would not escape destruction unless they returned to God.

God deliberately sent Ezekiel, a young preacher during the course of his training, to a post of grave danger. Ezekiel was indeed a prophet in perilous times. In addition to calling Ezekiel to preach and prophesy, God also called him to be a "watchman."

Consider the role of the watchman. The watchperson's task is to look over the landscape and alert the city to any approaching danger. The watchperson assures that robbers do not steal the crops before their life-sustaining grains have been harvested and stored in barns.

God likewise needs a watchperson. God did so then and does so now. God needs a watchperson—not a politician, not an economic analyst, not an intellectual lightweight, not a mere reader of Scriptures or reciter of prayers. When the government has little sense of God, when the nation is overcome with institutional greed and moral madness, when the flag waves higher than the cross, and when war is peferred over peace, God requires a watchperson!

The watchperson is of no value, however, unless he or she can see. The watchperson God wants and can use must possess vision. The watchperson must see in order to protect against the sword.

What of the sword? The sword is both figurative and literal. The sword is anyone or anything that has the capacity to bring death. History will be replete with swords. The names of Osama bin Laden, Saddam Hussein, and George W. Bush will be heard when that roll is called. That's a sword. The World Trade Center and the Pentagon—symbols of our economic and military might—were brought crashing to the ground by terrorists. Clearly someone is wielding a sword. Our government is pursuing international terrorists while arrogantly forgetting the terrorism the world has suffered at America's hands. In this milieu where the sword is an ever-present reality, God requires a preacher, a prophet, and a watchperson who can see what lies ahead and speak to it in God's name.

The Lonely Leader

Textbooks reveal the interconnectedness of leadership and vision, yet they often fail to relay the truth that visionary leadership comes with a price. That price is loneliness. One who bears God's Word and dares speak God's vision must be prepared for a life of loneliness. The experience of loneliness is particularly acute when one believes that he or she is on assignment as an ambassador of the King, to use the apostle Paul's analogy, and is the only one called to the task.

Perhaps one of the greatest longings of persons in the gospel ministry is to draw a crowd. We who preach spend our whole lives in search of a crowd. We understandably want to be like Jesus, who preached to five thousand (more if the women and the children had been counted!). We measure our church's "success" by our ability to attract a crowd. We keep track of our number of members, because numbers bring legitimacy to our ministry and tend to guarantee that we will be surrounded and thus be the center of attention week by week. If we are the center of attention, we must be wanted and needed. If we are wanted and needed, then surely we must be loved. This, however, is not always the case.

To be true to his or her call, God's preacher-prophet-watchperson must be aware that loneliness comes with the territory. In fact, the watchperson, by definition, is in a perpetually lonely situation, for a watchtower cannot hold a crowd. Being a watchperson requires the ability and the willingness to stand alone. It feels lonely to stand and speak when others will not hear; to preach when those in the pew do not understand; to proclaim a vision of God that others cannot see; to preach, like Ezekiel, to dead people, church members whose Sunday morning apathy surpasses a comatose state and who aren't even aware that they are dead.

Yes, you have a God-given vision that must be preached to dead people who cannot hear; who can no longer shout; and who will not bow their heads, clap their hands, pat their feet, or say, "Amen." Preach your vision as you must, realizing all the while that your task will be to open the doors of the church for dead people to come in. Without a doubt, the leader who is also a watchperson faces loneliness at every watch.

There is a loneliness, however, that is far greater. Loneliness for the preacher-watchman is most striking because it is most internal. This loneliness is one that friends cannot erase and for which congregational families cannot compensate. It is a kind of existential loneliness coming in the darkest part of the night and forcing us to meet the ambiguities of life. To struggle with the self that cannot be expressed is to be lonely. To struggle with the tension of calling and purpose, knowing all the while that what you wish to be is at odds with what God requires you to become, is to be lonely. To stand in that strange and eerie place where you used to hear from God, where He used to show up but now is undeniably absent and silent, is to be lonely. So then, it appears that because I have this calling and this vision, I am condemned to be lonely—believing, at the same time, that by God's promise I am never alone. It is the very essence of faith. It is a conundrum. It is the price of visionary leadership.

The Futile Pursuit of Popularity

Moreover, a watchperson is often disliked. When God gave instructions to Ezekiel, God warned him that even after Ezekiel had blown his trumpet, preached the Word, declared the vision, and warned the nation of the dangerous sword, the people still would not believe him. Yet God did not absolve Ezekiel of his responsibility to speak. God requires that a visionary watchperson declare what he sees whether or not those to whom he speaks believe it. If the preacher does not blow the trumpet, does not sound the warning, does not expose the vision, not only will the people die, but the preacher will be held personally responsible for their deaths. The preacher is in a proverbial catch-22.

Unfortunately, the preacher-watchperson who effectively carries out his or her assignment will never win a popularity contest. In fact, no "true preacher" can be a popular preacher. The prophet-watchperson who brings good and bad news can never be assured of the fleeting commodity of popularity. If the preacher declares "the whole counsel of God"; "reproves, rebukes, and exhorts with all longsuffering and doctrine"; and uses the gospel as a two-edged sword, cutting as it heals and healing as it cuts, that preacher can never be popular.

Perhaps that is as it should be. For if a vision is to have integrity, if a vision is surely the uncompromised word of God, whether or not that vision makes one popular does not matter. God does not need a preacher who has been marginalized and compromised by city hall or the purveyors of earthly power. God does not need a preacher who can be bought and sold. God does not need a watchperson whose ethics are in conflict with his or her appetite. God does not need a watchperson who makes people feel good. God needs a preacher who is sure of the calling, who is not afraid to be lonely, and who scorns popularity in order to be faithful. That's the only kind of watchperson God is calling for in "these last and evil days."

Prophetic Laryngitis

Finally, the vision for the church can only be cast and claimed if the one to whom the vision is given is not afraid to preach. "Prophetic laryngitis" prevents many a watchperson from declaring the Word that God requires. The only thing worse than a preacher who *will not* preach is a preacher who *cannot* preach. The preacher who cannot preach is one who has become frightened by enemies both seen and unseen. When fear sets in, ministry is muted when it has a duty to speak.

God gives visions that are hard for the watchperson to handle and hard for the people to see. Those to whom the vision is preached may not want to see or hear. That's part and parcel of the process. So, if in your hour of meditative reflection, you discover that you are unwilling or unable to perform the function required of you, find another place to be silent. At this critical juncture of the church's life, there is no place for cowardly watchmen or watchwomen!

The work of the watchperson-visionary is too vital to be compromised. The hungry and the homeless are dying on street corners. Speak, watchperson!

The blood of our children is running in the sewers and the streets. Speak, watchperson! Death no longer comes as a "thief in the night"; it comes as a high school rampage or a sniper's bullet by day. Speak, watchperson!

The church is failing to live up to its commission to bring men and women to more abundant life. Speak, watchperson!

As long as you claim to have a vision from God, you will never be popular and you will never escape from the imperative to preach. Speak, watchperson!

The task of the visionary watchperson is both dangerous and vital. Nevertheless, our commitment to the church of Jesus Christ means that we can never escape its pain and peril. We can only be assured of its reward.

Although the fig tree shall not blossom, neither shall fruit be in the vines; the labour of the olive shall fail, and the fields shall yield no meat; the flock shall be cut off from the fold, and there shall be no herd in the stalls: Yet I will rejoice in the LORD, I will joy in the God of my salvation. The LORD God is my strength, and he will l make my feet like hinds' feet, and he will make me to walk upon mine high places. (Hab. 3:17–19)

How to Handle Life's Trials

When Community Is in Conflict
Romans 8:35–39

> Who shall separate us from the love of Christ? shall tribulation, or distress, or persecution, or famine, or nakedness, or peril, or sword? As it is written, For thy sake we are killed all the day long; we are accounted as sheep for the slaughter. Nay, in all these things we are more than conquerors through him that loved us. (Rom. 8:35–37)

I am convinced that whenever any preacher stands before the sacred desk, he or she experiences a certain sense of dread and foreboding. A heaviness saturates both soul and spirit, making climbing the pulpit stairs a seemingly endless and painful journey. Coming to the place of preaching means coming to a place where joy and sorrow meet. Coming to the hour of preaching means coming to that hour when humanity and divinity are joined together. Coming to the time of preaching means coming to that time when unuttered prayers are still in search of eternal answers. Yes, there is no doubt in my mind that whenever a preacher stands before the sacred desk, he or she does so with a sense of dread and foreboding.

Perhaps this is so because the very nature and context of preaching requires that some "issue" is addressed, an issue that is often a source of conflict between Christ and culture. We come to hear the preaching of the gospel because our lives are filled with conflict and issues. It doesn't matter who we are, whenever we enter the house of God, we drag our issues with us.

Thus, if any preaching moment is to be truly authentic, it must be watered by tears and stained with blood. We who are among the "Calvary crowd" know that our road is never easy; the pathway is never plain. We are always climbing up the rough side of the mountain. And so this word addresses an issue that affects us as a congregation both personally and collectively.

As you know, our church has been the subject of both television and print media stories about the conflict over our use of the Garrison school yard for parking on Sundays. In my estimation, the coverage of this conflict has been biased against us in that it has favored those who object to our using the Garrison school yard. Our side of the story has never been told. Allow me, therefore, to set the record straight by telling the story from the church's perspective.

In August of this year, the church applied for an extension of its one-year lease to use a portion of the Garrison School property for Sunday parking. The lease was opposed by the Area Neighborhood Commission (ANC) and several community residents. They opposed the lease because they wanted to renovate the play area to create a ball field for the area's children and had found funding from a philanthropic contractor to do so. They did not want the church to park on the remaining area of the field that would not be consumed by the renovated portion.

Despite the opposition, the DC Public Schools approved a one-year lease for parking on the field one day per week for the sum of $5,000. The church was also required to continue providing in-kind support services to supplement the school (for example, an after-school program). Metropolitan subsequently paid the full lease amount and gave an additional five thousand dollars for instructional support of the teachers and students at Garrison School.

Prior to the current conflict, Metropolitan Baptist Church had, without incident, parked on Garrison field for the twenty-two years of my tenure and even before I became pastor. Garrison and Metropolitan have enjoyed a mutually supportive relationship that has served as a model for church-school collaborations in this city and in the nation. The church has sponsored cross-cultural trips for students, created a special after-school life-skills development program designed specifically for Garrison School students, provided bus services for field trips, contributed food to Garrison families, opened the church facility for the school's use for special events, and supported the school and its faculty and staff in numerous other ways.

Over the last five years, the church has contributed gifts and services to Garrison School worth more than $210,000 over and above the $5,000 annual lease. Unfortunately, the media chose not to inform the public about the positive contributions we were making to the community through our support of Garrison School. Instead, the church was pictured as an unfriendly neighbor who sought to deprive the community's children.

We scheduled several meetings with city representatives, the school's principal, and a school parent to seek an amicable solution to the problem. Following these discussions, we accepted an offer of compromise by the superintendent of DC Public Schools that would provide a playground and ball field for the children and limited parking for the church.

After the compromise was announced, the community once again voiced its opposition and obtained a temporary restraining order to prevent the church from parking on the yard pending the outcome of a court hearing.

The question for us is: How do we proceed? First of all, let's be clear about what the real issues are. The first real issue before us has little or nothing to with parking or playgrounds. It has to do with a shift in our culture that attempts to demonize the sacred. We seem to have reached a point where God no longer has a place in our cities and communities. Yale professor Louis Dupre has written,

"The west appears to have said [a] definitive farewell to a Christian culture. . . . The [Christian] faith has been absorbed by the culture and has become simply another cultural artifact. Christianity has become a historical factor subservient to a secular culture rather than functioning as the creative power it once was."[1] Dupre's statement speaks to the fact that this generation is not concerned about God, Jesus, the church, or church folk.

Second, this conflict involves a racial shift in the community that has been brought on by new residents who seem determined to take control of a community we have inhabited for more than one hundred years. Our new neighbors don't seem to desire to collaborate, cooperate, or even converse.

Third, this conflict involves the status of longstanding community institutions within changing neighborhoods in Washington, DC. While the influx of affluent, mostly white people into inner-city communities may improve the community's prominence and raise property values, the new residents do not appear to share the values, interests, and concerns of their older, mostly African American neighbors. The black church has been a vital part of the life of most African American communities since the early nineteenth century. Treating the only institution that has consistently supported the welfare of black Americans with such apparent disdain dishonors our history and our contributions and risks the continued polarization of our neighborhoods.

Fourth, be assured that Metropolitan is not alone in this struggle. Churches elsewhere in the District and throughout the nation are experiencing the same kind of struggle in their communities. That explains why so many churches are moving to newer, more receptive locations.

What seems to be happening in this situation is familiar ground. I've been on this street before. And I say with a sense of righteous indignation that we've come too far to turn around. The days where we are beholden to those who have controlled us in the past are over.

The familiar spiritual says, "Before I'll be a slave, I'll be buried in my grave and go home to my Lord and be free."

The Assignment

Now that the underlying issues are on the table, the question remains: How shall we proceed? What are we going to do to bring this issue to closure?

There are several primary concerns we must address. First, although we are not a party to the suit, any decision reached will have both a short- and long-term affect on us. Second, intervening in the lawsuit would be time-consuming and emotionally, spiritually, and financially draining. Third, even if we intervened successfully, we do not stand to gain much, because shortly after we received the new lease, it was amended from an annual lease to a month-to-month lease, which can be terminated at any time.

Is it worth it to us to maintain a month-to-month lease that would be subject to continual challenges for the right to park in an area that doesn't sufficiently meet our parking need in the first place? Is it worth it for us to incur legal bills in the process and risk the possibility that the media will continue to tarnish our reputation in the community over this matter? On the other hand, we stand to lose much. If we intervene, we stand to lose the parking altogether even though it isn't sufficient. We also stand to lose a measure of our historic reputation and credibility while gaining increased animosity from a portion of the community. And we lose the ability to make a decision for ourselves before the court makes one for us.

How, then, given all these variables, shall we proceed in a manner that is consistent with the Word of God? Before answering this question, I must first, as pastor and undershepherd of Christ, understand my role in this process. Thank God, I know why I am here. I am here on kingdom business with kingdom priorities. It is not my assignment to lead you into valleys but to encourage you to climb high mountains.

My task is not to lead you into paths of useless confrontation; my task is to lead you in paths of righteousness. My assignment is to preach the Word of God to the people of God on the way to the city of God. My assignment is to "reprove, rebuke, exhort with all longsuffering and doctrine" (2 Tim. 4:2).

Like Jeremiah, my assignment is "to root out, and to pull down, and to destroy, and to throw down, to build, and to plant" (Jer. 1:10). My job is to "seek . . . first the kingdom of God; and his righteousness," and everything else I need will be added (Matt. 6:33).

Jesus has some direction for us:

> When they persecute you in this city, flee ye into another: for verily I say unto you, Ye shall not have gone over the cities of Israel, till the Son of man be come. (Matt. 10:23)

> If any man will sue thee at the law, and take away thy coat, let him have thy cloak also. (Matt. 5:40)

> Agree with thine adversary quickly, whiles thou art in the way with him; lest at any time the adversary deliver thee to the judge, and the judge deliver thee to the officer, and thou be cast into prison. (Matt. 5:25)

> Love your enemies, bless them that curse you, do good to them that hate you, and pray for them which despitefully use you, and persecute you. (Matt. 5:44)

The Bible also has a word for the adversary:

> Be not deceived; God is not mocked: for whatsoever a man soweth, that shall he also reap. (Gal. 6:7)

And the Bible has a word for me:

> And whosoever shall not receive you, nor hear your words, when ye depart out of that house or city, shake off the dust of your feet. (Matt. 10:14)

What we face today has the capacity to divide our community and our church. I refuse to permit that which polarizes our community to polarize us. I refuse to permit those who stand outside of this house to bring a contentious spirit of dis-ease into God's house. I refuse to let anything or anybody separate us from God, our history, our heritage, or one another. I refuse to let racism make me a racist.

I refuse to let those who hate me cause me to hate them. I refuse to let those who are unneighborly make me become unneighborly. I refuse to major in minors. I refuse to waste my time worrying about cars in a parking lot when my assignment is to be concerned about sheep in the pasture. I refuse to confine the church to an ecclesiastical bathtub when the "old ship of Zion" was designed for deeper waters. I refuse to permit Metropolitan to close this century fighting over parking when there are homeless people to be fed, outcasts to be clothed, homes to be healed, and sinners to be saved.

Therefore, effective immediately, the Metropolitan Baptist Church membership will no longer park on the Garrison School grounds. As a matter of principle, however, because we will not permit those who just came into this community to be the sole say-so in what happens in this community, and because we will not permit anyone to discount or disrespect the people of God, and because Metropolitan Baptist Church has a legitimate stake in this community, our legal counsel will be instructed to file a motion to intervene in the matter of the temporary restraining order that is pending before the DC Superior Court. No other legal proceedings in this matter will be pursued. By proceeding in this manner, we will limit our financial expenses. It is my prayer that the courts will decide in our favor, thereby upholding the right of all community stakeholders to access public space. Regardless of the lawsuit's outcome, however, Metropolitan Church will no longer use the space.

Advice from the Apostle

Now that we have addressed our collective trial as a church, let's take a look at how we can handle our own life's trials. Paul's writings are instructive. In his letter to the church at Rome, Paul reveals his own experiences with trial and tribulation and examines and defines the great "watchwords" of our faith. He writes with awesome detail of his own understanding of the righteousness of God. Paul stands in the priestly and prophetic tradition to give direction to Jews and Greeks, wise and unwise. He addresses such weighty matters as sin and salvation, sanctification and justification. Paul defines what it means to be a church as well as the importance of preaching within it.

In addition to all the knowledge he eloquently displays in Romans, Paul also shows that he knew what it was to have trials. Paul knew what it was to be converted, but he also knew what it was to go blind on the road to Damascus. Paul knew what it was to be admired for his charisma and charm, but he also knew what it was to walk with a limp, to have a "thorn in the flesh" that he called the very messenger of Satan. Paul knew what it was to sit in great institutions of higher learning, but he also knew what it was to be beaten by rods, deserted by friends, shipwrecked, lied about, and called everything but a child of God. Surely Paul knew what it was to have trials.

A close examination of the book of Romans reveals that the first reason Paul had trials was because he was busy doing something for the Lord. Trials do not come to those who are not doing anything. Spiritual warfare comes only to those who actively engage in doing the things of God. If the only thing the church does is Sunday morning worship and midweek prayer meeting, you can be sure that Satan will not come against that church.

But when folks' lives start changing, Satan gets upset. When alcoholics throw away their bottles; when drug addicts put down their needles; when husbands stop beating wives and homes start getting stronger; when men are taken out of the mission and off of park benches and given jobs and respect; when the church decides that it's not enough for children to run, that they need to read; when the church decides it's not enough for little black children to go to the basketball court, that they need to be trained to go to the Supreme Court; when the church decides to start a school that teaches children about Jesus and gives them technological skills, critical thinking skills, and foreign language skills, Satan gets upset.

Romans 8 instructs us that there is a way to handle life's trials. First, we must have the right perspective. In verse 18, Paul says, "For I reckon that the sufferings of this present time are not worthy to be compared with the glory which shall be revealed in us." Paul was well aware that it was all a matter of perspective.

When you are standing in the middle of your trials, tribulation, or difficulty, whatever you want to call the "mess" you are in, remember that God is not dead. He's still got the whole world in His hands. Your situation is not as bad as you think it is. The world is not coming to an end. The bottom is not going to fall out. The sky is not going to fall. God is not dead.

I used to think that what Paul meant in this passage was that I had to wait through the night in order for joy to come in the morning. Then I discovered that every time morning comes, joy comes with it.

Every time the sun comes up—joy!

Every time light chases darkness—joy!

Every time I wake up—joy!

Every time I get up—joy!

I don't have to look for it, it's coming whether I look for it or not—joy!

You can handle life's trials if you have the proper perspective. You need more than perspective, however. You also need purpose. In Romans 8:28, Paul wrote, "We know that all things work together for good to them that love God, to them who are the called according to his purpose." Things do not just happen. Things happen according to God's purpose.

The people of Israel did not know why they had to cross the Red Sea, but God had a purpose.

Joshua did not know why he had to march seven times around the walls of Jericho, but God had a purpose.

Elijah was insulted that he had to receive his food from ravens, but God had a purpose.

Jonah did not know why he had to live three nights in the belly of a fish, but God had a purpose.

Likewise, God has a purpose for the conflict we face. "Maybe God is trying to tell us something," we say.

Maybe God's got a brighter and better world.

Maybe God has some plans for us that He will reveal in His own time.

Whatever the tragedy, whatever the trial, whatever the tribulation, all you need to do is remember that God has a purpose for it. Regardless of whether I can understand it, can explain it, or think I can handle it, Paul said, "All things work together."

And they work together because, whatever the process is, it's perfecting His purpose. Whatever is going on in your life, He's perfecting His purpose in you. Whatever is going on at your job, your home, or your church, He's perfecting His purpose in you.

"All things work together for good to them that love God." Good is the purpose. If all things work together for our good, we must love God. Through the sickness, through the pain, through the ups, through the downs, in the valley, on the mountain, with friends or no friends, we must love God.

To be able to handle your trials, you not only need perspective and purpose, you also need power. This is the source of that power: "If God be for us, who can be against us?" (Rom. 8:31).

If God be for us, it doesn't matter that the hordes of hell are at our door.

If God be for us, He has ten thousand angels at His command.

If God be for us, "why should I feel discouraged and why should the shadows come?"

If God be for us, the Lord is my light and my salvation, whom shall I fear?

If God be for us, when my enemies and my foes come upon me to eat up my flesh, they will stumble and fall.

If God be for us, no weapon formed against me shall prosper, and every tongue that shall rise against me in judgment God will condemn.

If God be for us, we have power!

One final word of instruction on how to handle life's trials: Declare victory before the battle is over! The *Washington Post* asked me, "Reverend, now that there's an injunction against you, what are you going to do?" Well, I've got an answer. I'm going to declare victory before the battle is over!

How, you ask, does victory become ours before the battle is over? The psalmist suggested that in spite of one's circumstances, in victory and in apparent defeat, it is always appropriate to praise God for what God has done in anticipation of what God will do. This, then, is our plan. This is how we will handle this time of trial. In the presence of apparent defeat, let's praise Him!

> Praise ye the LORD. Praise God in his sanctuary: praise him in the firmament of his power. Praise him for his mighty acts; praise him according to his excellent greatness. Praise him with the sound of the trumpet: praise him with the psaltery and harp. Praise him with the timbrel and dance: praise him with stringed instruments and organs. Praise him upon the loud cymbals: praise him upon the high sounding cymbals. Let every thing that hath breath praise the LORD. Praise ye the LORD. (Ps. 150)

Let the praise begin!

Homecoming Sunday
September 19, 1999

Already!

The Power in the Preface

Exodus 1:1 – 5

Vision casting requires, among other things, an indomitable faith in God's ability to provide beyond your ability to see or to make sense of your circumstance. Few visions, if any, emerge with all the necessary details in place. The authenticity of a vision does not rely on human understanding or the human ability to make the vision come to pass. Where there is vision, God makes provision.

And all the souls that came out of the loins of Jacob were seventy souls: for Joseph was in Egypt *already*. (Exod. 1:5)

Serious readers know the importance of reading the preface of any writing. The opening words of any treatise are far more than meaningless introductory chatter. The opening words are quite literally a *pre-face*, or a way of looking at the "face" of what has been written before actually encountering the substantive text. The opening words are intended to introduce the reader to the broad concepts that form the intellectual foundation for the writing. They are designed to set the mental course for the reading and establish the historical or personal point of view from which the author begins.

Thus, like the prefaces in any writing, prefaces in the Bible are important. Any serious study of Moses' second book, Exodus, requires that the reader pay attention to the opening words. At first glance, the words seem to be mired in genealogical gibberish containing unknown names with difficult pronunciations. Greater meaning lies beneath the surface, however. In particular, it must be noted that the preface to the book of Exodus begins with the word "Now," indicating that the book is not intended to stand alone, but is unquestionably the author's way of connecting something that had been written before. "Now" can imply any number of things. After something has happened in the past, "now" is used to refer to the present. "Now" can indicate the interrelatedness of concepts and ideas or illustrate how one thing follows another.

How is the word "now" used at the beginning of Exodus? Even someone with limited biblical knowledge knows that Exodus follows Genesis. The book of Genesis records the creative activity of God through a series of "God-events." For instance, Genesis reveals the God-event of the creation of humankind through the lives of Adam and Eve. We learn of their assigned tenancy and subsequent eviction from the Garden of Eden and what it would take for them to be able to make their way back to the garden.

Genesis also reveals the God-event in the life of Noah, who was instructed to build a boat while living in the middle of a dry and barren desert. It further records the God-event in the life of Lot, who was saved from the destruction of Sodom, but whose wife was turned to a pillar of salt because she dared look back. And Genesis also reveals the God-event in the life of Abraham and his wife Sarah, who, though bent, withered, and gnarled by age, received a promise that God would bless their seed and give them a son, Isaac, who would cause their name to be blessed among the nations. Isaac fathered Jacob, and Jacob fathered twelve sons, among them his favorite son, Joseph.

Abraham's genealogy is important to understanding the preface to the book of Exodus. Genesis 43 notes that "the famine was sore in the land" of Israel (v. 1). Consequently, Jacob sent all of his sons, with the exception of Benjamin, to Egypt to buy grain in an effort to avoid certain starvation and inescapable death. From the closing lines of Genesis to the preface of the book of Exodus, all the sons of Jacob had died and 350 years had passed. Thus, the writer of Exodus penned a preface that reads:

> Now these are the names of the children of Israel, which came into Egypt; every man and his household came with Jacob. Reuben, Simeon, Levi, and Judah, Issachar, Zebulun, and Benjamin, Dan, and Naphtali, Gad, and Asher. And all the souls that came out of the loins of Jacob were seventy souls: for Joseph was in Egypt already.

This genealogy of Israel serves to remind us that whenever we are exploring what God is doing or straining to see what God will do, we must remember what God has already done. The use of the word "Now" in the preface to Exodus implies that a history has gone before that must not be ignored. This is a history we cannot escape.

"Now" is the word of connection. "Now" is the word that reminds us that we are where we are because of what God has done for us in the past. "Now" is the word that reminds us that we cannot appreciate where we are until we first remember where we used to be and who helped us get where we are.

In the book of Exodus, the writer is set to divulge God's activity on behalf of the people of Israel while they were in Egyptian bondage. He cannot begin telling the story, however, until he prefaces it by acknowledging the contributions of those who have gone on before.

The listing of important names shows a full appreciation of history. One of the tragedies of this generation is that our children (and a whole lot of adults too!) do not know the names of persons who have made significant contributions. They do not remember that such contributions to their lives were even made. They don't *remember* the names because they don't *know* the names.

Whenever black people gather together, somebody ought to remember the names! Phillis Wheatley, Benjamin Banneker, Richard Allen, Nat Turner, Henry Highland Garnet, and Frederick Douglass. Remember the names! Harriett Tubman, Sojourner Truth, Booker T. Washington, Henry McNeal Turner, Mary Church Terrell, Paul Lawrence Dunbar, James Weldon Johnson, Ethel Waters, and W. E. B. DuBois. You cannot tell the story of our history until you remember the names! Marcus Garvey, Langston Hughes, Zora Neale Hurston, Adam Clayton Powell Jr., Marian Anderson, A. Philip Randolph, Paul Robeson, Rosa Parks, Martin Luther King Jr., and Malcolm X. We must remember the names!

Let's tell our young people that it's all right to talk about Shaquille O'Neal, but don't forget Goose Tatum and Meadowlark Lemon and the other Harlem Globetrotters who could not play professional basketball because they were African American. While we're listening to Toni Braxton, we must also read Toni Morrison. While we celebrate Venus Williams, we can't forget Althea Gibson. Celebrate Sammy Sosa, but don't forget Satchel Paige, Willie Mays, Larry Doby, and Roy Campanella. While sitting in your corporate office with your name on the door making a six-figure salary, don't forget those who made bridges out of their bodies so that you could be where you are. We can neither escape nor forget our connection with history. That's why we must remember the names!

Remember Joseph

The five short verses of this preface not only reveal a history we cannot escape, they also reveal a forgiveness we cannot live without. All of the names in the verses represent Jacob's sons. The names also represent Joseph's brothers, who hated Joseph because he was loved most by his father, who had given him a coat of many colors.

These were the same brothers who stripped Joseph of his coat, threw him into a pit, and left him there for dead.

These were the same brothers who sold Joseph to some passing Ishmaelites for twenty pieces of silver, which is how Joseph arrived in Egypt in the first place.

These were the same brothers who, because of their treachery, placed Joseph in such a vulnerable position that he wound up in prison on trumped up charges of sexually abusing Potiphar's wife.

Joseph's life had been in a shambles because of his brothers. Through his experience, Joseph knew that sometimes the people who will mess you up most in this life are the ones who are closest to you. The ones who will take advantage of you, destroy your life, ruin your credit, eat up your food, wear your clothes, run through your money, and ruin your reputation are not your enemies; they are your brothers and sisters!

Despite all that had happened in the past between Joseph and his brothers, they are still included in the preface: Reuben, Simeon, Levi, Judah, Issachar, Zebulun, Benjamin, Dan, Naphtali, Gad, and Asher. All the brothers are there. They are included because, although they sold Joseph into slavery (see Genesis 37), Joseph forgave them (see chapter 45) for their past sinful deeds. These verses remind us that everybody needs to be forgiven. There are relationships that cannot continue until somebody says, "I forgive you." There are marriages that are headed for the divorce court unless somebody says, "I forgive you." When you read the preface to the book of Exodus, don't forget that Joseph's brothers are listed because Joseph forgave them of their past deeds. This is a forgiveness neither you nor I can live without.

The introductory verses also show us that we need to know that God is working whether we see it or not. It is worth noting that in this particular passage God's name is not mentioned. In the opening verses, we find history, genealogy, Jacob, and Joseph, but no mention of God. It seems as though God is not involved.

Yet in Genesis 45 and 50, Joseph provides the basis for his ability to forgive:

> Now therefore be not grieved, nor angry with yourselves, that ye sold me hither: for God did send me before you to preserve life. For these two years hath the famine been in the land: and

yet there are five years, in which there shall neither be plowing nor harvest. And God sent me before you to preserve you a posterity in the earth, and to save your lives by a great deliverance. (45:5–7)

Genesis 50:20 goes on to say:

But as for you, ye thought evil against me; but God meant it unto good, to bring to pass, as it is this day, to save much people alive.

Through his experiences, Joseph discovered that even during life's bleakest moment when God appeared to be absent, God was there. Just at the moment when Joseph thought he had been abandoned, God was preparing a positive outcome from what appeared to be a negative circumstance. All of us have had experiences that have caused us to feel that God is not present. In your life and mine, there appear to be incidents or accidents in which we don't feel God's presence at all. But I have come to understand that what we think is an accident is really a "God-cident," an opportunity for God to be glorified through our circumstance.

When it appears that your life has turned upside down, look for God in it. When it appears that you are so far down that there is no way up and no way out, look for God in it. When it appears that everything you saved is lost, everything you were holding has slipped away, everything you thought was positive has turned out negative, every time you have gotten up somebody has knocked you back, everything you were depending on has let you down—when your world turns upside down, look for God in it. He's there.

When you can't see Him, He's there.

When you can't find Him, He's there.

When you don't know where He is, He's there.

When you feel all alone, He's there.

When you stand alone in the dark, He's there.

When there is no one to help, He's there.
When there is no hope, He's there.

> *Truth forever on the scaffold,*
> *wrong forever on the throne.*
> *Yet that scaffold sways the future,*
> *and beyond the dim unknown,*
> *Standeth God within the shadows*
> *keeping watch above his own.*

James Russell Lowell

Calling Israel Out

These first five verses may not look like very much yet, but there's power in the preface.

The book of Exodus, meaning "the way out," records the experience of the children of Israel as they were coming out of bondage on their way to a new land and home. Today God is calling His children "out." It is important to note that after four hundred years the children of Israel had become comfortable with their circumstances in Egypt. They had become satisfied slaves who had learned to accommodate themselves to an unwholesome situation. Yet God had to call them "out" from where they were in order to guide them to the place He intended for them to be. God is always calling Israel "out." Likewise, God is always calling the church "out" in order to bring the church back in.

The writer uses these first five verses to remind the children of Israel that whatever their experience was, others had experienced the same thing before them. If God was calling Israel out of Egypt, it is because God had first called Israel out of Israel. By doing so, God not only intended to get Israel out of Egypt, He also wanted to get Egypt out of Israel. God was calling these people out of Egypt not to experience something novel or uncommon, but something that somebody else had already gone through. Therefore, the writer names those who have already been where they are going.

It's refreshing to know that no matter what your circumstance, somebody has already "been there and done that."

You're not the first one to have hard trials, tribulations, sickness, or distress.

You're not the first one to climb up the rough side of the mountain, through hills and valleys.

You're not the first one to navigate through rough seas and high water.

You're not the first one to make it through dangers seen and unseen.

You're not the first and you won't be the last.

If somebody else has made it, you can make it.

Whatever it is that God is calling you to do that you've never done before, you can make it.

Whatever burden you've been called to bear that you've never had to bear before, you can make it.

We serve the same God of Israel.

If Israel could make it, you and I can too!

If Reuben could make it, I can make it.

If Simeon could make it, I can make it.

If Judah could make it, I can make it.

If slaves could make it, we can make it.

If those who could not read or write can make it, we can make it. Our parents had to learn from books with ripped out pages.

If they could make it, we can make it. Our ancestors got medicine from tree bark and never saw a doctor. We can get medicine from CVS, and we have doctors all over town.

If they could make it, we can make it.

You can make it; you can make it.
That trial you're going through—
God's gonna show you what to do.
You can make it; you can make it.

Shirley Caesar

The reason we can make it is found in verse 5: "And all the souls that came out of the loins of Jacob were seventy souls: for Joseph was in Egypt *already.*"

If you look over in Genesis 43, you will discover that "the famine was sore in the land" of Israel. To survive the famine, Jacob sent his sons to Egypt, with the exception of Benjamin, to buy corn so as to avoid certain starvation. By reading the closing lines of Genesis through the preface of Exodus, we find that all the sons of Jacob had died and 350 years had passed. But when the writer looked back over the exodus of the children of Israel, he concluded that when they reached Egypt, *"Joseph was in Egypt already!"*

Likewise, whenever you are at a place where you cannot sufficiently meet your need; whenever you are called upon to leave the known for the unknown; whenever God bids you to leave one place and go to another; whenever God disturbs where you are and sends you off in search of where He wants you to be, you need to know that before you get there, God has provided for you already!

This God of the exodus provided for Israel before Israel even knew they had a need. Sometimes it is difficult to understand *why* God does what He does or *how* He does what He does. As God allowed to happen to Joseph, God can allow your brothers to tear the clothes off your back, hate you, throw you in a pit, and sell you into slavery. He may allow you to wind up in prison and suffer hunger, deprivation, and pain in a foreign land. Through all of that, you may think God has let you down when, in fact, He has picked you up. You may think God has disappointed you when, in fact, He has appointed you and made you prime minister of the people who intended to be your master and keep you enslaved. You think God has "dissed" you, but in reality He has honored you by putting you in charge of the food in a time of famine. God put Joseph in such a critical place in Egypt that when the sons of Jacob arrived there, God had provided for everything they would need *already.* Just as soon as Israel had decided to leave Israel, God had dispatched the resources Israel would need before Israel arrived.

In the same way, God will provide for your needs before you know you have needs. Theologically speaking this is called the *fore-knowledge* of God. Philosophically speaking it is called the *a priori activity* of God. Logically speaking it is known as *providential causality*—God causes things to be before things are known to have been caused. God intervenes *beforehand* so that what we need is already *on hand.* This is the prior action that occurs before prior action is needed. God always acts in the realm of the "before."

Before the hills in order stood—

Before the earth received her frame—

Before the mountains were brought forth—

Before there was a whence or a where, a when or a whither—

Before the morning stars sang together or the Sons of God shouted for joy—

God acts before so that when we get where He intends for us to be, the work is done *already.*

The verse, which suggests that Joseph was in Egypt already, not only speaks to the fact that Joseph was already physically there, it also means that the things that Joseph and his brothers would need were there *already.*

When God told Noah to build an ark, Noah couldn't see it, but the flood was there *already.*

When Moses stood on the banks of the Red Sea, the power to part the waters was in his hand *already.*

When David stood before Goliath, he didn't need to go to the store, because the slingshot and stone he needed were in his pocket *already.*

When the three Hebrew boys were thrown into the fiery furnace, they discovered that they were not there by themselves; a fourth person who looked like the Son of God was there *already.*

When Elijah told the widow of Zarephath to open her empty cupboard, the meal and the oil were there *already.*

And just as God was already there in these circumstances, God is already working out your circumstance.

If you don't know how you got the job you have, it's because God had made a way *already*.

If the doctors don't know how you walked away from the hospital, it's because the Chief Physician was there *already*.

If you thought you didn't have enough collateral to get a mortgage for the house you're living in right now, God had opened the door for you to get a loan *already*.

When you look back at some problem you thought impossible to face, you'll see that the reason you're smiling today is because God raised up some friends for you, gave you some allies, sent somebody to stand by your side. Make no mistake, the help you needed got there before you got there because God was there *already*.

You were looking for the bottom to drop out, but God was there *already*.

Your were looking for all hell to break loose, but heaven broke loose instead; God was there *already*.

You should have been dead right now, but God has been keeping you alive, and He's right by your side *already*.

You don't always get what you want when you want it. But when you have gone through something, God fixes it so that when you have learned your lessons in the school of hard knocks, when you have matured to the point that you can handle what you're asking for, by the time you get ready for God, God has been ready for you. In fact, He has already done what He said He would do. He has made a way. He has opened doors. He has put bread on your table, clothes on your back, and shoes on your feet. He has sent friends to your aid.

We walk by faith and not by sight because God has gone ahead of us and already done what we need Him to do.

He leads me in green pastures and beside still waters. He restores my soul. He anoints my head with oil. My cup runs over. It's already done.

When I need angels to watch over me and bear me up in their hands, it's already done.

When I need a counselor, I already have one.

When I need a friend, Jesus sticks closer than a brother. It's already done.

"There is therefore now no condemnation to them which are in Christ Jesus." It's already done.

"Whosoever shall call upon the name of the Lord shall be saved." It's already done.

"The prayer of faith shall save the sick." In fact, it's already done.

"If you have faith as a grain of mustard seed, ye shall say unto this mountain, remove hence to yonder place: and it shall remove; and nothing shall be impossible unto you." It's already done.

"Though your sins be as scarlet, they shall be as white as snow; though they be red like crimson they shall be as wool."

What about my sin?

> *Jesus paid it all. All to Him I owe.*
> *Sin had left a crimson stain; He washed it white as snow.*

It's already done. What about my sin?

> *What can wash away my sin?*
> *Nothing but the blood of Jesus.*
> *What can make me whole again?*
> *Nothing but the blood of Jesus.*

It's already done. What about my sin?

> *There is a fountain filled with blood*
> *Drawn from Emmanuel's veins.*
> *And sinners plunged beneath that flood,*
> *Lose all their guilty stains.*

It's already done. Whether you know it or not, God has blessed you already!

"Already" proved to be a prophetic word, indeed. Once the congregation bought into the vision of relocating the church and expanding the ministry, we had no idea where we would move. The likelihood that we would find a location within our Washington community was remote, because there were few available parcels that could accommodate us or that were economically feasible. Just as with Abraham, God would need to show us the country in which to dwell.

Three months later God manifested His working in an envelope on my desk. That same week I was the subject of a Washington Post *article entitled "An Exodus with an Unhappy Genesis." Even though we had neither purchased land nor had prospects for the purchase of land in the suburbs or anywhere else, the* Washington Post *writer assumed that we would relocate the church to the suburbs.*

When I returned to my desk that memorable Thursday in March, I found an unsolicited package of materials from a local real estate agent indicating that he had a client who had property that might be suitable for our new place of worship. Moreover, the available parcel, consisting of thirty-four acres located a mere twelve miles east of our current location, was already zoned for church use. Its infrastructure included a paved road and access designed for heavy traffic flow; curbs, gutters, fireplugs, and streetlights; and a water management system already approved and maintained by Prince George's County. On top of that, plans had already been approved for two new subway stops less than one mile from the site. As a result, access would be simple even for our members without cars. More than that, the parcel was located in the county that was home to at least one-half of our current members. Homes were located close enough that prospective new members could actually walk to church!

God had located the land, introduced the land to us, and offered it at a reasonable price. Furthermore, there were two three-story office buildings for sale with ample parking on both sides of the street by the available land. This property immediately became the work space for the Metropolitan Community Development Corporation, and the entire complex was named "Miracle Plaza"! God is faithful. When He gives a vision, He makes provision.

When the Praise Is Over

Facing Life's Bitter Waters

Exodus 15

*B*e careful with praise. Praise can be seductive. Praise can put you *in a spiritually euphoric state that will lead you to believe that things are better than they are. If you are led to such a state, it is quite possible that you will reach a point of malaise and depression when the praise is over. Despite our best efforts the church does not live in a perpetual state of sunshine. Things do not always go well. The proclamation of our victory often occurs in the presence of our defeats.*

Then sang Moses and the children of Israel this song unto the Lord, and spake, saying, I will sing unto the Lord, for he hath triumphed gloriously: the horse and his rider hath he thrown into the sea. And when they came to Marah, they could not drink of the waters of Marah, for they were bitter: therefore the name of it was called Marah. And the people murmured against Moses, saying, What shall we drink? (Exod. 15:1, 23–24)

At its core, Exodus 15 is an exuberant psalm of praise. If ever there were a people who had an experience that gave them an opportunity for demonstrative, extravagant praise, surely it was the people of Israel. If ever there was a people who had a collective story to tell about God's redemptive activity, surely it was the people of Israel. If ever there was a people who could see for themselves a living example of God's bounteous grace, if ever there was a circumstance in the whole of human history that undoubtedly showed the salvific hand of divine intervention in human affairs, surely it was the people of Israel. And so, when the people of Israel considered their present position in relation to their prior plight, they could not help but get caught up in ecstatic and joyful praise.

The reason for Israel's joyful praise is familiar to most. Israel had moved from dire straits to an even worse situation. Famine swallowed up Israel. Crops failed. Vines bore no fruit. The streams, brooks, and rivulets dried up. Sheep had no grass in which to graze, for pleasant pastures had turned from fertile green to barren brown.

In response to this desperate situation, Jacob sent ten of his twelve sons to buy grain from Egypt. When Jacob's sons arrived in Egypt, they found their brother Joseph, whom they had sold into slavery, "living large" in Pharaoh's palace, second only to Pharaoh himself, and responsible for allocating food supplies.

After 350 years had passed and all of Jacob's sons had died, "there arose up a new king over Egypt, which knew not Joseph" (Exod. 1:8). For the next four hundred years, the new king "set over them taskmasters to afflict them with their burdens. . . . And . . . made the children of Israel to serve with rigour: and they made their lives bitter with hard bondage, in mortar, and in brick, and in all manner of service in the field: all their service, wherein they made them serve, was with rigour" (Exod. 1:11, 13–14).

Then somewhere in the backstreets of Goshen, a baby named Moses was born. God sent a baby who Pharaoh said should not live but whom the midwives would not kill. God sent a baby in the bulrushes of a little creek on the edge of the Nile. Then God, in the middle of the river, arranged for a cross-cultural, interracial adoption process that permitted an Israelite whom Pharaoh was trying to exterminate to live in Pharaoh's home, eat at Pharaoh's table, dress in Pharaoh's clothes, and learn from Pharaoh's tutors.

But now, after four hundred years of slavery, God determined that enough was enough. The Bible says, "God heard their groaning, and God remembered his covenant with Abraham, with Isaac, and with Jacob" (Exod. 2:24). Now God sent that same Moses to stand at the seat of Pharaoh to plead, "Let my people go." A burdened people were then able to throw off the shackles that had so long held them in the ignominy of their captivity.

And so, as we reach Exodus 15, we find the people of Israel after they had crossed the Red Sea. As they stood on the threshold of a land God had promised, they joyously recited what God had done.

> I will sing unto the LORD, for he hath triumphed gloriously: the horse and his rider hath he thrown into the sea. (v. 1)

> Pharaoh's chariots and his host hath he cast into the sea: his chosen captains also are drowned in the Red Sea. (v. 4)

> And with the blast of thy nostrils the waters were gathered together, the floods stood upright as an heap, and the depths were congealed in the heart of the sea. (v. 8)

> Thou didst blow with thy wind, the sea covered them: they sank as lead in the mighty waters. (v. 10)

> For the horse of Pharaoh went in with his chariots and with his horsemen into the sea, and the LORD brought again the waters of the sea upon them; but the children of Israel went on dry land in the midst of the sea. (v. 19)

They told their story over and over again. And they did so in song. They rehearsed what God had done and how He had brought them out. Moses sang every word of the song. In fact, Exodus 15:1–19 is known as the Song of Moses. These verses represent the jubilant, ecstatic praise of Moses and the children of Israel.

Moses was not alone in showing his jubilation. When Moses was finished, his sister, Miriam, took over. The praise was so high and lasted so long that Miriam lost her poise and sophistication, took a timbrel in her hand, and "all the women went out after her with timbrels and with dances" (Exod. 15:20). With Moses and Miriam singing and the women dancing, high praise surely had engulfed the camp.

Given what they had been through, high praise was understandable. They truly had something to shout about. But some would say all this shouting was a bit excessive. Surely all they needed to do was mention God's accomplishments once and be done with it. Yet two-thirds of this chapter records the rejoicing, singing, and shouting about what God had done.

Today some would say that contemporary praise practices are excessive. Sometimes the praise just goes on and on. It seems like the shouting will never come to an end. Sometimes it looks as though the shouting and the dancing have no rhyme or reason. That's why some people will lean over and whisper, "It doesn't take all that."

Well, I believe that it does "take all that." When you realize how far the Lord has brought you, it takes "all that." When you realize how far inside the ghetto you were, how deep in the swamp you used to be, and how the Lord pulled you out and lifted you up, it does take "all that." When you realize just how far down in the water you were, when you realize how close you came to drowning, when you realize that nobody but the Lord lifted your feet out of the miry clay and set your feet on a rock to stay—yes, it does take "all that."

The redeemed of the Lord ought to say so. Where the Spirit of the Lord is, there is liberty. When you recognize all that God has done and know that if you had ten thousand tongues to sing, you still couldn't praise Him enough—yes, it does take "all that"!

I am not at all puzzled by Israel's praise. What does puzzle me, however, is the stark contrast between Exodus 15:1–21 and verses 22–24, which say: "So Moses brought Israel from the Red Sea, and they went out into the wilderness of Shur; and they went three days in the wilderness, and found no water. And when they came to Marah, they could not drink of the waters of Marah, for they were bitter: therefore the name of it was called Marah. And the people murmured against Moses, saying, What shall we drink?"

In the first twenty-one verses, we find Israel shouting. In the very next verse, however, we find the same people murmuring because they were thirsty. That sounds a lot like church folk.

As long as the Israelites could see the way, they shouted. Yet just as soon as the way got a little hard and the road got a little rugged, they murmured.

As long as everything was prepared for them, they shouted. But just as soon as it looked like they would have to exercise their own ingenuity and use their own determination, and as soon as it looked like they would have to rely on a vision that was not their own, they murmured.

As long as they had what they wanted, they shouted.

As long as their needs were being met in the way they wanted them to be met, they shouted.

As long as things were certain, plans were set, and the destination was sure, they shouted.

But just as soon as the water ran out, their attitude changed. Just as soon as things were not going the way they thought they ought to be going, the climate in the congregation changed. Just as soon as it appeared that appropriate travel arrangements had not been made, they took their eyes off the Lord and tried to get rid of Moses. Just as soon as it looked like there might be some danger or difficulty ahead, the praise was over!

Bitter Water

Let's look at what happens when the praise is over. Upon examining this text, several realities about life become clear. First and most obvious is that every life is marked by *bitter water*. When the children of Israel got to Marah, they discovered that they could not drink the water there because it was bitter. They were thirsty, but the water was polluted. Their throats were dry and their lips parched, but the water was contaminated.

This may not be a very comforting thought, but we must realize that life is filled with bitter water. I wish I could tell you that your life will always be sweetness and light. I wish I could tell you that life is "a bowl of cherries" or "a bed of roses" or that you will always be able to "tiptoe through the tulips."

Life can give you some bitter water. Life can give you some "hard pills to swallow," "throw you some curves," or "set you back on your heels." We all know that life's best lessons are taught in the "school of hard knocks." In this life, you will have tribulations. Yes, there is some bitter water in life.

When the thing you've planned for falls through or when the thing you've given your life for fails to come to fruition, that's bitter water.

When you discover your child is using drugs and you don't know how it happened, that's bitter water.

When the marriage you dreamed of and planned for winds up in court for the nastiest of divorces, that's bitter water.

When your body insults you with a sickness for which you were not prepared and the doctors say they can't help you, that's bitter water.

"Bitter water" will surely present itself. The question is: What will we do when it comes. Will we—

Spend our time talking about how we have been victimized by the water?

Complain that nobody has to drink bitter water as we do?

Castigate the leader as though the leader made the water?

Find somebody else to blame for the condition of the water?

Put on our victim clothes and walk around saying "the man" made us drink bitter water?

Complain that some evil and pernicious racist scheme condemns us to forever drink bitter water?

Or will we pick ourselves up, stop being victims, find a new relationship, stop polluting our water, stop corrupting our own environment, learn the scientific formula for purifying water, and then clean up the water for ourselves? God cannot help you unless you are willing to help yourself.

The problem in this text is not really with the water. In fact, God did away with the problem by simply throwing a tree into the water, which sweetened it. The bitterness of the water was no longer an issue.

The real problem here, which is evident by the shift from the shouting to the murmuring, is *sickness in the sanctuary*. The text says, "If thou wilt diligently hearken to the voice of the LORD thy God, and wilt do that which is right in his sight, and wilt give ear to his commandments, and keep all his statutes, I will put none of these diseases upon thee, which I have brought upon the Egyptians: for I am the LORD that healeth thee" (Exod. 15:26).

Whenever there is an unnatural shift from shouting to murmuring, you can be sure that underneath it all is an element of sickness. When God brought Israel out of Egypt, He did so after giving signs—most prominently the plagues that would consume the land. One of the signs was the turning of the rod into a snake. The snake is a symbol of Satan. Whenever there is confusion about whether to shout or complain, Satan is somewhere lurking. And whenever Satan is present, sickness is not far behind.

God sent ten plagues in all. First, water turned to blood; then frogs covered the land and even invaded Pharaoh's bed and ovens. The dust became gnats and filled the air. After that there were flies, plagues on the livestock, boils on animals and humans, hail that destroyed crops, locusts that devoured what the hail left, darkness over the land of Egypt, and the death of the firstborn.

While these plagues were intended for the Egyptians, I believe that when Israel stopped praising and started murmuring, this indicated a deficiency in their spiritual immune system that made them susceptible to the same kinds of diseases that victimized Pharaoh. The sickness began in Pharaoh's house, and Israel had reached a point where the same plagues that visited Pharaoh's house were about to visit them. It is possible to live so close to people that you catch their diseases.

On the other hand, not all sickness in the church begins on the outside; some sickness comes from within the church.

There are some "psychotic flies" in the church.

There are some "neurotic gnats" in the church.

There are some "schizophrenic frogs" in the church.

There are some hellions that raise "hail" in the church.

Once praise stops and turns to murmuring, sickness is allowed to enter. But thank God that where there is sickness, we do not have to remain in that condition, because there is also an opportunity for healing.

I see a number of interpretations of this text. One suggests that we don't have to be sick: "If thou wilt diligently hearken to the voice of the LORD thy God, and wilt do that which is right in his sight, and wilt give ear to his commandments, and keep all his statutes, I will put none of these diseases upon thee . . ." (Exod. 15:26). As long as I remain faithful in my relationship with God, none of these diseases will be put on my life. Some sickness I cannot avoid because I am a mortal person made of flesh and blood, but there is other sickness that I can avoid simply by being in a right relationship with my Creator.

And so I come to church because I know there is an opportunity for me to be healed. Authentic worship has therapeutic value in that it leads to individual and collective healing.

When I come to church, I'm not seeking anything on the surface.

When I come to church, I'm not seeking a momentary catharsis.

When I come to church, I'm not seeking a spiritual placebo that will trick me into thinking I'm better off than I am. Rather, I'm looking for someone to diagnose my situation and prescribe the medicine that will put me on the path to spiritual health. When Jesus met the crippled man at the pool of Bethesda, He asked: "Wilt thou be made whole?" (John 5:6). Likewise, when you go to church, expect Jesus to be ready to heal you, to turn your life around.

Don't come in here if you don't want your life turned around.

Don't get in this water if you don't plan to go out of here better than you were when you came in.

When I come to church, I want to get in the healing water. I'm looking for a shower of blessings. I'm looking for a balm in Gilead. I'm looking for a healing for my body and a healing for my soul. I want to tell somebody, "Whereas once I was blind, now I see." Like the woman with the issue of blood, I want to touch the hem of Jesus' garment. I want my head anointed with oil and my cup running over. I don't come to shout just for the sake of shouting; I come to shout in anticipation of and as a consequence of my healing.

The bitterness of the water—which was, in part, the precipitating cause for their murmuring—was indicative of an internal deficiency in Israel's spiritual immune system that showed up as a virus and then became the full-blown disease that revealed the fact that there was sickness in the sanctuary. In spite of the apparent spiritual sickness, God says you do not have to be sick. None of these diseases will come upon you if you remain in proper relationship with the God who brought you out. Therefore, the text not only implies that you have an opportunity for healing, but you must remember to remain open to a relationship with the one who is the source of the healing.

There is no healing apart from the healer. God says that if there is going to be any healing in your life, any purpose in your praise, any healing of the sickness in the sanctuary, you need to be aware of the one who is doing the healing. This is what He says: "I am the LORD that healeth thee." This is the only place I know of where the name Jehovah-Rapha can be found. It means that God has charge over the healing process.

I know you are impressed with genetic cloning. I know you are amazed by scientific advancement with the human genome that enables people to unravel the mysteries of the human genetic footprint. But beyond our amazement, we must know that God is the one who created the genome in the first place. What we are trying to do is get to where God has already been. "I am the LORD that healeth thee." I may not understand cloning or the human genome thing, but I do understand that when I get sick, God comes and brings my medicine to my room. Slaves sang it this way:

> Come on in de' room.
> Come on in de' room.
> King Jesus is my doctor.
> He writes out all my 'scriptions.
> He brings me all my medicine in my room.

I do understand that Jesus is a doctor who has never lost a patient. I do understand that He has more medicine in the hem of His garment than any drugstore in town. I do understand that He has healing in His touch.

But what do you do when the praise is over? If you are still asking that question, it is because you have not read the last verse of chapter 15. God threw a tree in the water and dismissed the water problem, and the Israelites kept walking. They came to Elim where there were twelve water wells and seventy palm trees. They had berries and palms, and they camped by the water.

Now then, if you want to know what to do when the praise is over, look for the wells. When the Israelites got to where they were going, God had already provided not just one well, but twelve wells of water. Before they got there, the wells were already there. So when it looks like you can't shout anymore, look for the wells. When it looks like the waters in your life have become bitter, look for the wells. Whatever you need, God will provide.

Look for the wells. There is yet hope in a dismal situation.

Look for the wells. They are the sign and signature that God has been where you are headed.

Look for the wells. They are the imprimatur of a God who keeps His word and provides for your every need.

Look for the wells. He promised to lead you to green pastures beside still waters.

Look for the wells. The God who leads you *through* the water is the same God who leads you *to* the water.

He is faithful to His promise!

DO YOU SEE WHAT I SEE?

The challenge of every pastor-watchman is to make sure that those whom he or she leads are able to see the vision of God just the way he or she sees it. The great temptation of the pastorate is to believe that our vision is the only one. We alone have visions of authenticity . . . or so we would like to believe.

To the contrary, I believe we may be missing the mark. The challenge before pastors is to clearly understand and internalize the challenge that God has placed before them. To understand the challenge is more difficult than it may seem. Your visions may multiply—one vision leads to another. The challenges will be numerous and may be political, economic, social, psychological, or spiritual, and they may have numerous implications that are difficult at first to discern. Stated differently, your visions will create complexities in your ministry for which you are totally unprepared.

Pastors (I among them) are famous for knee-jerk reactions. With Bible in hand and glibness of tongue we are ready to speak on any issue with full confidence and authority that we know what we are talking about and with great incredulity that others do not know and see as well. The lesson I have learned, however, is that the vision will wait. The vision will wait for the right time . . . for God's time. What is required is full introspection, critical analysis, and spiritual downtime to permit the pastor-watchman to know and to respond to God's call in meaningful ways.

In other words, take the time to get ego out of the way. Take the time to be sure that you are in step with the Eternal. If your vision is authentic, if the will of God for you and your ministry is clear, you will not be harmed by the generous use of time. "The vision," says Habakkuk, "is for an appointed time." *You* must not appoint that time. You must be willing to put the process of appointment in God's hands and then be available to respond at God's direction. Moses could not get Israel out of Egypt until he first got Moses out of Moses. Never fear. Never forget. We serve an on-time God!

PREACHING
the VISION

—————— PART II ——————

THE STATE OF THE CHURCH

E *ach year it is my practice to give a state of the church address to share with the congregation the significant accomplishments of the past year as well as my vision for the church's future growth and development. This address also provides the congregation with an opportunity to be informed about significant issues that we face and to be given a sense of where the church leadership stands both administratively and spiritually. My 2001 state of the church address held particular significance because it was delivered in the wake of the church's decision to move the church to a location in suburban Maryland.*

The decision to relocate the church into suburban Maryland was not an easy one. After all, Metropolitan has been in the heart of Washington, DC, for almost 140 years. Moreover, we had built a new building a little over ten years ago. Not long after we built, it became evident that despite our best efforts at strategic planning, the building we had constructed was inadequate for our growing ministry. We discovered that we did not have enough rooms to accommodate students for Bible study and discipleship classes. While we were adding members to the church at an incredible pace, we found that we could not adequately meet their needs because of limited space. In many ways, it was a blessing, not a problem. The church was too full; the pews were too short.

Church growth and inadequate parking alone were not sufficient warrants for the relocation and expansion of the Metropolitan ministry. But the parking challenge was real, since we were in a neighborhood that was saturated with churches. Simply stated, a church cannot survive if the congregation cannot gather. Our challenge, in my view, was not church growth but church decline. We were beginning to see a decline in terms of both new members and people who opted for other ministries that were better equipped to serve their needs. The decline was caused by numerous factors.

First, the church was beginning to attract a different clientele or customer base. It was becoming readily apparent that families with children brought increasing expectations of the church, its ministries and its facilities. Convenient parking was only one requirement. There was also the need for children's activity space, adequate classrooms, and an atmosphere conducive to a wholesome lifestyle for the church.

Second, the church had become a commuter congregation. Fewer than one percent of the congregation lived within the church's zip code. We were dramatically failing in our efforts to attract our new neighbors to worship or to church activity.

Third, we gave serious attention to the possibility of alternative worship experiences at times other than 11 o'clock on Sunday morning. In the end, we did not pursue this alternative, primarily because we believed we would further antagonize and alienate the community already burdened by the parking problems.

Fourth, and perhaps most important of all, is the fact that the church building is 140 years old. The historic significance of the ground itself as well as the sacred space upon it is not inconsiderable. While not always vocal, the congregation had great feeling and emotion attached to this plot of ground. To suggest abandoning this location for another was the cause of great angst for many members.

To the chairs, the officers, and the leaders of the board and ministries of this body of Christ, I greet you in this one hundred thirty-seventh year of our organization and in the twenty-fourth year of the ministry that you by God's grace have permitted me to share.

Grace, mercy, and peace from God the Father, God the Son, and God the Holy Spirit be with you all.

It is with a deep sense of thanksgiving and divine urgency that I come to this sacred desk to share with you the "state of the church." From time to time, I have stood in the place of our fellowship and praise to speak about the ministry that God has given to us—our problems and potential, tears, triumphs, all.

These are serious days for our church. As we move toward the erection of a new temple for our Christ, it is critical that as we change our direction and focus we do so in the right way and with the right spirit. The way we respond to change—whether we maintain a Christian spirit of unity and love and a willingness to lead and to follow—will determine in large part whether we succeed or fail.

Today I speak to you from a pastor's heart, clear in my own spirit about the direction God has for us. At the same time, I am sensitive to the issues and concerns that are in your hearts and on your lips. Twenty-four years ago this congregation voted to give me the authority and responsibility of leadership—a responsibility to which I have sought to be faithful. I have not been perfect or faultless during my tenure, yet I have always sought to act out of an abiding faith. In my role as pastor-teacher-servant leader, I come asking for your ear but more especially to ask for your understanding, love, and hearts.

Pillars of Our Work—from the Inside Out

Metropolitan has expanded its ministries in ways that are worthy of your interest and support. During the last three years, we have formed three nonprofit corporations that will allow us to extend our work into the community. We have begun IAMA, Inc. (*iama* being the Greek word for "healing"), a counseling ministry designed to bring help and hope to persons in crisis, in need of a listening ear or a helping hand. Our counseling ministry allows us to nurture others to the knowledge that maturity and freedom are the inheritance we hold as children of God.

This year more than seventy-five students are enrolled in the Metropolitan Day School, which serves prekindergarten to fifth grade. Metropolitan Day School is not a charter school that relies on government support. Rather, it is a private Christian academy supported solely by the church for its support beyond tuition. With a curriculum designed to prepare children to succeed in a global society, our school uses technology and innovative instructional techniques to help students develop critical thinking skills and their God-given creativity. By God's grace, Metropolitan Day School will become one of the finest faith-based educational facilities in this area. However, the school needs your continued support if it is to be successful.

Finally, we developed the Metropolitan Community Development Corporation. This corporation is designed to involve the church in the development of low and moderate-income housing, senior citizen living facilities, and other projects that will assist redevelopment efforts in the District of Columbia and Prince George's County, Maryland. Each of these corporations, IAMA, Inc., the day school, and the Metropolitan Community Development Corporation, is understaffed and undercapitalized. We greatly need your continued financial and prayer support.

Faith-Raising: The Substance of Things Not Seen

By far, the most critical issue that we now face and will face for the next several years is the construction of a new tabernacle for the living God.

I am aware of the concern many of us have regarding this issue. Our current building on R Street is our church home. Many of us were reared here. On this soil, many of us met Christ as Savior, were baptized, were married, dedicated our children to the Lord, or laid our loved ones tenderly to their rest.

I have blessed memories of this place as well. Twenty-four of my thirty-five years in Christian ministry have been spent in service to Metropolitan. I watched the footers as they were poured and the foundation as it was laid, and I listened while others said I had dug a hole but would never fill it. To borrow a phrase from Winston Churchill, my "blood, sweat, and tears" are in this place and in this church.

Because we have an attachment to this place, all of us are going through a period of grieving. When the decision was first reached to build in a new location, many of us denied that such a thing could actually happen. As the reality of the decision and its impact on our lives becomes more and more apparent, for some the grieving process has lead to sorrow and even anger and tears. Let me assure you that I understand your pain, for I too have shed tears.

Nevertheless, in 1999 we embarked on a journey to assess our future at this location. For one year, we held church town meetings, conducted focus groups, and used surveys to sample opinion. After that process was complete, I came before you to give an account of the vision that God had laid on my heart.

In that meeting, a clear and substantial majority of members voted to pursue three courses of action. First, the congregation consented to relocate the church to an undetermined location. Second, the church voted to authorize the board of trustees to recommend suitable land for relocation. In March of 2000, suitable land was found, and in April of 2000, the church voted, nearly unanimously, to authorize the purchase of thirty-four acres of land in Largo, Maryland. Third, we voted to sell the church's current property.

Having said all that, let me attempt to address any lingering concerns. The relocation of this or any other church is the most sensitive issue that any congregation can address. The decision can create anxiety because it requires a move from the secure to the uncertain, from the known to the unknown.

It is clear that we have fully outgrown this facility. Every person and ministry of this church has been affected time and time again by the inadequacy of this space. It is also clear in every respect that this neighborhood is different from the one in which Metropolitan was built and grew. We are simply unable to continue to grow in this location. There are ministries and outreach programs that are begging to be born but cannot be simply because of our space constraints. We know that parking is and will continue to be a major factor that also militates against the continued growth of this church.

And we also know, in our heart of hearts, the process through which we have gone to reach our decisions and come to our conclusions has been spiritually based, full, fair, and complete in every way.

Nevertheless, we are involved in birth pains. Metropolitan is being "born again" both literally and figuratively. Something new is about to come forth, and that has caused us to feel anxiety and pain. While the challenges we face are painful, they are God's way of keeping us humble and in touch with Him. The natural result of our labor, however, is a new and exciting creation that will reflect the very handiwork of God.

Let's join our hands and hearts to complete, in a spirit of love and harmony, the great task that God has given us. How we do that is just as important as what we do. I ask now that the loving and generous spirit of this congregation be released so that even passersby will look in upon us and say, "My, how they love each other; how they love their Christ."

We know that, like the children of Israel, God has given us the land. All we need to do is move forward and possess it. We know that the same God who has met us and protected us and sheltered us in this place will continue to do so wherever we are. The book of Deuteronomy says that God will bless us in the city and bless us in the field. Our mission is not serving ourselves; it is serving others in meaningful and productive ministry. We are not called to just meet our own needs but to leave a legacy for our children, a facility and a program in which their children and their children's children will be nurtured and grow in Christian love.

We have made a commitment to maintain a ministry in the District of Columbia despite moving to Largo. Our ministry will be what our name implies—we are Metropolitan, larger than location and more expansive than any confining plot of ground. We must never be limited by our heritage but propelled to greater service for Christ because of it. We must move beyond our fears and even beyond our anger and our grief to do something magnificent for God. A tiny group of men and women took a mere pittance from their pockets at a time of great national conflict and built an institution that outlived themselves. We can do no less. And we must begin from the inside out.

How does one build the church from the inside out? It can only be achieved through a faith-directed, spiritually sufficient strategic plan that touches every spiritual fiber of the church. Over the next few months, I will be sharing a ministry strategy that will shape our congregation's life for years to come. This strategy has a number of components. We will be involved in SpiritRaising, which challenges the church to a deeper and richer prayer life.

We will also be involved in FaithRaising, a process that will include pastor-led Bible study, thematic teaching in each of our Sunday school classes, and thematic preaching from the pulpit.

And we will design a program of LoveRaising that will ensure that every member of this congregation is touched by consistent and meaningful information distribution.

A serious component of our building process will be DiscipleRaising. We must raise up a generation of persons who are spiritually grounded and who bring both their professional expertise as well as their personal enthusiasm to the work of the church.

Over the next few months, I will be meeting with clusters of our ministries to assure a free flow of information between the pastor and those who are involved in the day-to-day work of the church.

Metropolitan is blessed in that we have persons in this congregation who have gifts and talents that are nothing short of astounding. We must strive daily to keep our congregational family intact. We must never forget, however, that "the harvest is plentiful." God has work for us to do, and there are enough hands here to do it.

Finally, our new program will include what I call WitnessRaising. The church must have a clearly definable program of evangelism that reaches the many communities in which our church is engaged. Our primary evangelistic emphasis must be in Prince George's County, our new home.

Building the Church: Upon This Rock!

Scripture records a conversation between Jesus and His disciples:

> When Jesus came into the coasts of Caesarea Philippi, he asked his disciples, saying, Whom do men say that I, the Son of man, am? And Simon Peter answered and said, Thou art the Christ, the Son of the living God. And Jesus answered and said unto him ... Thou art Peter, and upon this rock I will build my church; and the gates of hell shall not prevail against it. (Matt. 16:13, 16–18)

For years I have scoured the words of this text to determine their elusive meaning. Other prophets and preachers have sought to do the same. It occurs to me, however, that in His conversation with Simon Peter, Jesus is not simply building the church structure. Instead, He is really talking about building the church from the inside out.

There is a fundamental difference between what you must do to *fill* the church and what you must do to *build* the church. Jesus filled the church from the outside in, and in doing so, He never did His work in the synagogue; He always did it in the street. Jesus said that to fill the church, you need to go out into the highways and hedges and compel people to enter. Jesus believed that in order to fill the church, you need to gather men, women, and children on a hillside and feed them so they will come inside. Go find the folks who don't have anything and tell them they're going to be something. Go find the outcast folks and tell them they are the salt of the earth, a city set on a hill, a light that cannot be hidden. Be a good Samaritan to a man robbed by thieves. Look up blind Bartimaeus and tell him he's about to gain his sight. Touch a woman and heal her issue of blood. Touch a crazy man in a cemetery and leave him clothed and in his right mind. Touch human need anywhere you can. But you'll do it best from the outside in.

On the other hand, to *build* the church, you have to do it from the inside out. First, you must instruct the disciples. Jesus wasn't building a physical building; He was building up His followers.

James and John were hotheads. They needed building.

John Mark was a timid teenager. He needed building.

Matthew was a cheating tax collector. He needed building.

Judas was a liar and a thief. He needed building.

Jesus was so busy building up His disciples that He didn't have time to build a building. He knew that if He was going to build the church, He had to build it from the inside out.

Jesus had to let His disciples know that they were not the builders. Two things are apparent in Jesus' saying "Upon this rock I will build my church." First, He made it clear that *He* would build it. In effect, He was saying, "This process is not dependent upon whether you approve of it. I'll build it. It has my name on it, so I'll build it. I have the plans, which have already been approved. Since I am the architect of the universe, I get to decide what gets built. And I've decided that I'll build it."

The second thing Jesus was saying when He said that He would build the church was "It's my church. I'll build *my* church. It won't have your name on it. It's my church. It will have my cross on it because it's my church. Don't get too possessive. It's my church.

Don't get so proprietary. It's my church. The church was here before you got here and it'll be here long after you're gone. It's my church."

Jesus *fills* the church from the outside in, but He *builds* the church from the inside out. Jesus said one final thing regarding the church building business: "Upon this rock I will build my church; and the gates of hell shall not prevail against it." The reason Jesus builds His church from the inside out is because it has to be prepared for the "gates of hell." The text does not say that the gates of hell will not try to prevail. The text does not say that the imps of hell will not be on your trail. It just says that they will not prevail. If in the process of trying to build the church you discover that there's a little hell on the way, it means that you must be doing something right, because the devil is never happy when you try to build up the church.

God is getting us ready for a great church, and the devil is mad about it. God is getting ready to give us a "blessing on the beltway," and the devil can't stand it. God is getting us ready for another miracle, and the devil is out of his mind.

We know that despite all his efforts, the devil will not prevail, because "no weapon formed against [us] shall prosper." If the devil wants to fool around with weapons, I have my own weapons. I'm here wrestling with "spiritual wickedness in high places," but I have on the whole armor of God. I have on the breastplate of righteousness. I have my feet shod with the preparation of the gospel of peace. I have the shield of faith, the helmet of salvation, and the sword of the Spirit, which is the Word of God. And that's how we're building the church from the inside out.

Jesus said, "Upon this rock I will build my church." If He builds it, and if it is His church, that must mean the church building process is in His hands. Whatever it is you are doing, you need to understand the importance of it being in Jesus' hands.

A basketball in my hands is worth about $20, but a basketball in Michael Jordan's hands is worth $33 million. It just depends on whose hands it's in.

A baseball bat in my hands is worth about $6. But a baseball bat in Sammy Sosa's hands is worth about $19 million. It just depends on whose hands it's in.

A tennis racket in my hands is useless. But a tennis racket in Venus Williams's hands is worth a Wimbledon Championship and millions of dollars more. It just depends on whose hands it's in.

A rod in my hand will keep a wild animal away, but a rod in Moses' hands will part the waters of the Red Sea.

A slingshot in my hands is a toy, but a slingshot in David's hands will bring a mighty Goliath down.

Two fish and five loaves in my hands make a bad fish sandwich, but two fish and five loaves in God's hands will feed five thousand.

Nails in my hands will build something temporary, but nails in Jesus' hands will bring salvation to your soul.

It all depends on whose hands they're in.

Don't you worry; don't you fret; God is not through with us yet.

Whatever your worries, put them in His hand.

Whatever your doubts, put them in His hand.

Let the storm rage. I'm in His hand.

Let the wind blow. I'm in His hand.

You're in His hand. We're in His hand.

Building a tabernacle for the living God is an awesome undertaking, one that is doomed to failure if it is perceived as being human-directed rather than God-directed. My intention has not been to exalt church as a place over the church's purpose. Nevertheless, because the building of the church's physical structure has been so prevalent in my mind and in the minds of the congregation, it seemed important to consider the structure thoroughly in a biblical and spiritual context.

Thus, for several Sundays following my state of the church address, I preached a series of sermons from selected passages in the book of Exodus, specifically the passages regarding Israel's journey through the wilderness and God's detailed instructions for building the tabernacle. I believed that it was important that the sermons address the wilderness experience alongside the building of the tabernacle, because one led to the other. To consider the actual building process without considering what preceded the tabernacle's being built would have failed to give the subject appropriate attention. And if we inspected only the separate components of the tabernacle without viewing its meaning as an entire structure, we would have overlooked its full significance.

The intent of these sermons was to make implicit the purpose of the vision so that the congregation would not be overly concerned with what we were building while neglecting the greater purposes of ministry that would be served within the building. The aim of these sermons was to share with the congregation more than the fact that God had given us a vision, but that He had a reason and purpose for both our building the tabernacle and enduring the long and exhaustive process it would take to reach our God-directed destination.

The Tabernacle and the Testimony

Something to Say and a Reason to Say It

Exodus 25:8

And let them make me a sanctuary; that I may dwell among them. According to all that I shew thee, after the pattern of the tabernacle, and the pattern of all the instruments thereof, even so shall ye make it. . . . And thou shalt put the mercy seat above upon the ark; and in the ark thou shalt put the testimony that I shall give thee. And there I will meet with thee, and I will commune with thee from above the mercy seat, from between the two cherubims which are upon the ark of the testimony, of all things which I will give thee in commandment unto the children of Israel. (Exod. 25:8–9, 21–22)

Within Israel's history, few events compare, either in scope or effect, with the proceedings surrounding the design and construction of Israel's tabernacle. Some modern critics of the church believe that the construction of contemporary church structures is excessive and far too expensive. Yet you need only investigate the Word of God to discover the importance of the tabernacle to the Judeo-Christian tradition. Indeed, the building of the tabernacle consumes forty chapters of Scripture in the books of Exodus, Leviticus,

Numbers, and Hebrews. There you will find that God not only had a host of requirements in the tabernacle building process, He desired that those requirements be met by Israel, a wilderness congregation.

Israel had no membership roll; they were bound together by their blood. They had no prestigious members. In fact, they were the descendants of an assortment of Bedouin farmers known as Abraham, Isaac, and Jacob.

They had no padded pews to sit on. When they came to worship, they stood in the presence of the Almighty. Their place of worship had no address or zip code. They worshiped on mountaintops, in valleys, in desert places, and very often on rocky ground.

They did not come to worship dressed in their finest garb; they came with garments soiled and stained from rugged terrain. They came with marching shoes and sandals that had been worn bare. They came with the clothes of warriors, for they had either been in a battle or were headed to a battle.

When they gathered for worship, they had no choir or instruments to accompany them. They had "songs, hymns, and spiritual songs" that they composed on their journey to the Promised Land, a land that flowed with milk and honey.

In spite of the fact that they had no place to call home, these wanderers were charged with the arduous task of building an elaborate place of worship. It seems ironic that God would choose nomads who had nothing with which to build a tabernacle. Yet the tabernacle was built by these displaced and dysfunctional people who were in search of a place of spiritual mooring, security, and abiding permanence. The building of the tabernacle was therefore an experience of exile in the context of exodus.

The Tabernacle Context

Tabernacle building is never accomplished apart from a spiritual context. Such a building is always accomplished against a particular spiritual, social, or political backdrop. In this case, it was within the exodus experience that God required the children of Israel to build a tabernacle.

Tabernacles that God can use are always built out of a painful circumstance. Consider Israel's painful experience during its exodus. It was only after a famine rose in their land that the people of Israel ended up being enslaved in Egypt where they had gone in search of grain. It was only after God sent Joseph to Egypt and put him in charge of the Department of Agriculture that God began to open doors for Israel.

Then God met up with a murdering fugitive named Moses and gave him ministry instructions on Mount Sinai and a demonstration of His pyrotechnic powers in a bush that burned but was not consumed. Next God sent a stuttering and stammering Moses to stand in Pharaoh's court to declare, "Let my people go!" When Pharaoh refused, God sent the death angel in Egypt. But before the death angel got there, the Israelites put blood on their doorposts so that the death angel would pass over their homes and spare their firstborn children. Finally, God gave Moses a stick and left him standing in the middle of the Red Sea, so that with nothing but faith and a stick, the children of Israel crossed over on dry ground.

After all Israel had gone through, God ordered them to build a tabernacle. Ironic though it seems, in the context of the exodus experience, God sent a specific word from Mount Sinai through Moses about the building of the tabernacle: "And let them make me a sanctuary. . . ." He added something like this: "Moses, this is the assignment. In spite of what you have been through, burning bushes, Pharaoh, plagues, Red Sea crossing, murmurings and complaining, I'm telling you to make me a sanctuary."

God didn't seem to understand the type of people Moses was working with. These were poverty-stricken folks. These were "church folk" who did not understand their potential or appreciate how God sought to direct their future. Yet God told Moses, "Moses, let them make me a sanctuary."

God just doesn't get it, Moses probably thought. "Listen, God, these are church folk. Not only do they not have my vision, they don't have your vision. When I go to pray, they pout. When I talk about burning bushes, they think I've lost my mind. When I brought them your commandments from the mountain, they were not sure where I'd been. They can't agree on how to get from one mountain to the next, let alone how to take on a project of the magnitude you're talking about. These are worldly folk who seem more concerned about gold than they are about God. They want to build golden calves, something they can see and touch. They need a God that can be specifically identified and strategically located. While you're looking for praise, they're looking for a party."

Despite the challenges God knew Moses faced, God still said, "Let them make me a sanctuary." God's instructions were clear. He did not say, "Let them make *them* a sanctuary." He said, "Let them make *me* a sanctuary." When God gives instructions to build a sanctuary, you can be sure that He has not instructed you to build it for you. God has instructed you to build it for Him. It's not for your glory; it's for His glory. It's not so that by your achievement you can be exalted, but so that God will be exalted.

Careful attention must be paid to God's instructions for building a sanctuary. Notice that God said to Moses, "And let them make me a sanctuary; that I may dwell among them. According to all that I shew thee . . ." (Exod. 25:8–9).

God designed the building process. It was God's responsibility to show the people of Israel just what they needed in order to build the tabernacle. Israel did not need to fret over the building process, for God had already determined what the tabernacle was to look like before they began building it. God said, "I'll show you."

God has a reason for His sanctuary to be constructed in a particular way. God's instructions are never haphazard, impulsive, or ill prepared. Be assured that God always knows what He's doing. In this case, God's reason for having Israel build the sanctuary was clear: "that I may dwell among them." It's awesome to think about dwelling where God dwells. But it's even more awesome to think that God wants to dwell where we dwell.

You see, God is not homeless. God is everywhere. There is no place that God is not. God made the hills and the valleys. Every place is God's place. He hangs out with shooting stars at eventide and rides comets through the bosom of the night. He planted the oaks in the forest. He planted the weeping willows down by the riverside. Everything belongs to Him.

Yet God said to the people of Israel, "Let them build me a sanctuary that I may dwell among them." God wants to dwell among us too. God wants to live on your street. God wants His address to be your address. God wants to be where you can always find Him. God wants you to build Him a sanctuary so that He can dwell where you dwell.

But there's more here. Because the Israelites lived under circumstances of exile and exodus, they lived in temporary quarters. They were constantly on the move. But God wanted more than a casual relationship with them; He wanted a permanent relationship in a permanent location.

God's sanctuary is not about a structure; it's about a relationship. When I go to a building, I am simply going to a structure. The building can't bless me. The building can't heal me. The building can't make the pain go away. If I go to a place that is made with brick and mortar, I am merely going to a structure. On the other hand, if I go to a place where there is someone with whom I am acquainted, whose presence is dependable and reliable, and who does something for me every time I go, I do not go there because of the structure; I go because of the relationship.

Some people go to church because the building is beautiful. But a building's beauty won't hold you when the bottom drops out of your life. Other people go to church because they enjoy the choir or the preacher. But the choir can't save you and the preacher can't deliver you when all hell breaks loose in your house.

Some other people go to church because they meet their friends here or do some networking. But your friends may lie about you and scandalize your name. And I can assure you that the network you're counting on will let you down.

When you go to church, go because you have a relationship with God. Go because you want to converse with the great I Am. Go because you want to stand in the presence of the living God. Go because you want to meet up with the God of your salvation.

The importance of going to church doesn't have to do with bricks and mortar. It has to do with relationship. So, when I enter God's house, I enter because I know somebody there who knows how to anoint my head with oil so that my cup runs over; knows how to turn my water into wine; knows how to order my steps; knows how to hear my faintest cry; knows how to look beyond my faults; knows how to send angels to watch over me and bear me up in their hands.

God's Strategic Plan

If God asked the Israelites to build a tabernacle without giving them a plan for paying for it, He might be accused of being economically irresponsible. If God failed to assess the financial capability of the people to achieve such a task, somebody might say that He was deficient in strategic planning. But God never requires anything that He doesn't also provide the resources for. Exodus 25:1–2 says, "And the LORD spake unto Moses, saying, Speak unto the children of Israel, that they bring me an offering: of every man that giveth it willingly with his heart ye shall take my offering."

God's strategy for financing the building of the tabernacle was an offering. God didn't have a more sophisticated plan; He just asked for an offering. He did not say to raise money; He said, "Bring me an offering." He did not say, "Ask the community to give something"; He said, "Bring me an offering." He did not tell the Israelites to rely on the government to acknowledge them as "faith-based" so they could tap into government funding. All God wanted them to do was to bring an offering.

Let's see what the offering consisted of. Look at Exodus 25:3–7: "This is the offering which ye shall take of them; gold, and silver, and brass, and blue, and purple, and scarlet, and fine linen, and goats' hair, and rams' skins dyed red, and badgers' skins, and shittim wood, oil for the light, spices for anointing oil, and for sweet incense, onyx stones, and stones to be set in the ephod, and in the breastplate."

First, notice that God gave a long list of items that could be offered. It seems to me that God did this because He wanted to be sure that everybody had at least one thing on the list that they could bring. Nobody could talk about what they didn't have, because everybody had something to give.

Second, whatever Israel had was enough to do what God wanted. God gave a list of the things that would be needed for the building of the tabernacle. In addition to understanding that every-body had something to give and that what they had was enough to accomplish the task God had given them, we must recognize that everything Israel needed was already in the house. Israel did not have to look for outside resources to do what God was requiring of them.

Like Israel, if we want to build a tabernacle for the living God, we don't have to look elsewhere; what we need is already in the house. We don't have to make God appear to be a pauper by beg-ging, because what God needs is already in the house. We don't have to argue with each other about whether we can afford to do what God wants us to do. The hymn writer said, "All I have needed [God's] hand has provided." The resources are already in the house.

God told Moses, "Speak unto the children of Israel, that they bring me an offering: of every man that giveth it willingly with his heart ye shall take my offering" (Exod. 25:2). Clearly, a tabernacle for the living God cannot be built if the people have a stingy spirit. You have to bring your offering cheerfully with a *willing* spirit. Nobody should have to beg you to give.

Why should you and I be eager to give an offering to God? I don't know about you, but when I think of everything God has given me, it makes me want to give an offering to Him. An offering is not like the tithe. A tithe is something you are obligated to give; it already belongs to God. You have no choice but to give God what already belongs to Him. An offering is something you give because you want to.

When I think about the things God has given me, not out of obligation, but just because He wanted to, I can't help but bring my offering willingly.

In spite of my sin, God saved me; He didn't have to do it, but He did.

In spite of my filth, He cleansed me; He didn't have to do it, but He did.

When I fell down, He picked me back up; He didn't have to do it, but He did.

The doctors said I should be dead in my grave right now, but for some reason, God has kept me alive. He didn't have to do it, but He did.

When I remember the tight places in which I've been; the places I've been and I should not have been; the things I've done and I should not have done that I'm still here to talk about, I know that He didn't have to save me, but He did.

He woke me up this morning and started me on my way; He didn't have to do it, but He did.

I don't know about you, but I'm glad about it. That's why I bring my offering willingly.

Reasons to Build

There are two reasons the children of Israel were obligated to build the tabernacle. They can be found in Exodus 25:21–22: "And thou shalt put the mercy seat above upon the ark; and in the ark thou shalt put the testimony that I shall give thee. And there I will meet with thee. . . ."

Notice that God placed an ark—the ark of the covenant—within the temple. This chest made of acacia wood and covered inside and out with pure gold contained God's testimony. On the top of the ark was a lid covering made of pure gold that was called the mercy seat. At the end of the top of the ark were solid gold figures of cherubim.

The Hebrew word for mercy seat is *kapporeth,* which literally means "a place of covering for sin." On the Day of Atonement, the high priest, Aaron, would enter the Holy of Holies and sprinkle blood on the mercy seat, thereby making atonement for the sins of the nation of Israel. Once a year the high priest would atone for the sins of the nation with the blood of animals.

Unlike the people of Israel, we have the blood of Jesus. I'm so glad that one day on Calvary, Jesus paid the price for sin once and for all. I'm so glad that John could say, "Behold the Lamb of God, which taketh away the sin of the world" (John 1:29). I'm so glad that Paul could say, "He hath made him to be sin for us, who knew no sin; that we might be made the righteousness of God in him" (2 Cor. 5:21). I'm so glad that Jesus shed His atoning blood at one time to take away my sin and yours. The children of Israel had to build the tabernacle because they needed a place for atonement and a container for their testimony of what God had done in the collective life of the nation. Today you and I have our own testimonies.

Someone can say, "The Lord has been mighty good to me." Someone can say, "When I look back over my life and I think things over, I can truly say that I've been blessed; I've got a testimony."

And while we can bring our own testimony to the tabernacle, we still enter this tabernacle knowing that God promises to meet with us, for He said He would: "And there I will meet with thee." The Lord will surely meet you anywhere else, but there's something special about a Sunday morning meeting. When the saints of God gather, He will meet you there.

When the saints gather for a sweet hour of prayer, God will meet you there. When burdens press you down, God will meet you there. When storms keep raging in your life, when your heart is broken and you are bathed in despair, God will meet you there. Let us build a tabernacle. And let us build it from the inside out! And just as certain as God meets us where we are, God will surely meet us there.

THE TABERNACLE
AND THE VISION

Seeing the Church through God's Eyes
Exodus 25:8

And let them make me a sanctuary; that I may dwell among them. According to all that I shew thee, after the pattern of the tabernacle, and the pattern of all the instruments thereof, even so shall ye make it. (Exod. 25:8–9)

Vision is a key concept in contemporary management theory. Those who have management or leadership roles know that effective leadership requires vision. Without vision, a leader does not know where he or she is headed. Without vision, those who are asked to follow the leader cannot be sure they can trust the leader to steer them to a place they want to go. Vision sets the course. Vision determines the destination. As the saying goes, "If you can't see it, you can't achieve it." Thus, from the corporate world to the church world, vision is always a matter of vital concern.

The notion of vision and its importance is nothing new. When King Solomon wrote the book of Proverbs, his advice to leaders and followers was clear then and is clear now: "Where there is no vision, the people perish" (29:18).

But what is vision? While its importance is clear, its definition is not. For organizational theorists, vision is a hopeful image for the future; it is a standard for performance that provides direction for collective and unified effort. For management specialists, vision is what permits one to see a future that is more desirable than the present. Vision, then, always points to a realistic, credible, and attractive future.

Vision concentrates on the future. Vision is prospective rather than retrospective. Vision concerns itself with seeing what is ahead rather than dwelling on the past. Vision does not simply see things that are and ask, "Why?" Vision sees things that never were and asks, "Why not?"

George Barna will tell you that "vision creates the future." Vision defines the parameters in which and through which the future will emerge. Vision is "foresight with insight based on hindsight." Vision sees the invisible and then works to make it visible.

The Bible also speaks of vision. Daniel did not really understand who God was or what God was about until he "saw in the night visions, and, behold, one like the Son of man came with the clouds of heaven" (Dan. 7:13). That's vision.

God spoke to John the Revelator one day and declared, "Behold, I make all things new" (Rev. 21:5). And John saw it: "And I saw a new heaven and a new earth: for the first heaven and the first earth were passed away; and there was no more sea" (v. 1). That's vision.

John saw something else. "And I John saw the holy city, new Jerusalem, coming down from God out of heaven, prepared as a bride adorned for her husband" (v. 2). That's vision.

God's Vision and Ours

However vision is defined, it is clear that no one can lead effectively without it. I bring this to your attention primarily because I want to examine God's vision for building the tabernacle. When operating in the world of business, I am obligated to understand the corporate vision. I am obliged to understand how corporate strategy brings about long-term investor profitability. Similarly, if I am operating in the church and God is requiring me to build a church, I need to understand God's vision. I need to gain some insight in order to gain some foresight into God's vision for the future church.

If I discover that I am having difficulty understanding the purpose and the priorities of the church, it may be because I don't see what God sees. It could be that I don't have a God-centered and God-directed view of what God envisions for the church. My task is to abandon my vision and get in line with God's vision. Doing so will allow me to go where God is going rather than trying to get God in line with where I am going.

There is no question that God's vision is never easily seen. Stand for a moment in Noah's shoes: "Noah, I want you to build an ark. Even though you are standing in the middle of a desert, I want you to build a boat. Build the boat so that two of every animal in creation can get on board. It does not rain in the desert; you are nowhere near a body of water, but build the boat and tell your children to get on board. I have the specifications for you. I will tell you how many cubits by how many cubits. Even though you don't understand, just build the boat. You cannot see the future. You have no idea what I intend to do in your future. If I told you what was in store for your future, it would be too much information. You're not ready to handle what I have in store for your future. For the time being, Noah, all you need to know is, 'Build a boat.'"

God's vision is never easily seen.

Stand for a moment in Moses' shoes: "Moses, I want you to lead these people from slavery to freedom. Now, Moses, you need to know that I have been trying to get these people ready for this move for four hundred years and they still are not ready to go. They do not see what I see. Moses, this will not be an easy task. You must first convince them that they should follow you. You must convince them that out of all the people I could have chosen to lead them, I chose a stuttering ex-convict, a fugitive murderer, and a shepherd who has been tending stinking sheep for the last forty years of his life. They won't see the vision. Before they get out of town, they'll have to put blood on their doorposts so that the death angel will pass over their homes without killing their firstborn. Just as soon as they get out of town, death by Pharaoh's horsemen will be behind them and death by drowning in the Red Sea will be before them. I promise you they will not see the vision. Not only that, Moses, these people are hardheaded and stiff-necked. While you are praying, they will be playing. When you are talking about commandments, they will be thinking about building golden calves. They will grumble about their diet and get tired of the food and water I provide for them. Even though you tell them every Sabbath about a Promised Land—a land that flows with milk and with honey—they will prefer the cucumbers and leeks they used to eat. And, Rev. Dr. Moses, they will decide to get rid of you and go back to Egypt where they came from. They will not see the vision, because God's vision is never easily seen."

This biblical and historical review makes clear that every once in a while God requires something of us that we do not understand.

Vision is important to our lives today as well. Indeed, the issue of vision has no lasting meaning until it is addressed in one's own life. At some point, we all must ask ourselves questions like these: What is my vision, and is that vision consistent with God's vision for me? Where is the place of challenge in my life that God is requiring something of me that I do not understand? Where am I headed, and can I envision what things will look like when I get there? Am I just moving aimlessly from day to day and from week to week with no destination on my horizon, no sense of destiny in my soul, and no sense of purpose to my footsteps? What kind of future do I envision for myself? What are my hopes for the future? What thoughts shape my every waking moment? What am I striving for that makes it worth it to get out of bed every morning?

You ought to have a vision for yourself, because God has a vision for you. Jeremiah 29:11 says: "'For I know the plans I have for you,' declares the LORD, 'plans to prosper you and not to harm you, plans to give you hope and a future'" (NIV).

A person's vision must be aligned with God's vision. Thus, the moment God said, "Let them build me a tabernacle," the task of the people of Israel became to align their vision with God's vision. To truly understand the concept of aligning one's vision with God, you must understand the environment during the time in Israel's history when the vision appeared. Israel had left Egypt on a forced march with very little besides the clothing on their backs. They carried only what they could hold or pull on their carts. They were chased to the water's edge, and they entered the Red Sea by faith that God would hold the waters back. They wound up in the wilderness with no road map or satellite navigational system to steer them on their way. The only leader they had was an old man who stammered and stuttered when he talked, one who went off by himself for days at a time and came back talking about his encounters with God. The food was terrible, the accommodations awful. They were running out of everything. And there came the Reverend Doctor Moses saying that he had a vision from God that the people must build a tabernacle.

I can hear the people saying: "Wait a minute! We're already struggling, and you're talking about building a tabernacle. Wait a minute! We don't have a roof over our heads, and you're talking about building a tabernacle. Wait a minute! You haven't thought this thing through. You haven't done a thorough financial analysis. You obviously haven't considered the political ramifications of this rash decision. Folk come to church to be 'fed.' Folk come to church to hear the Word. They don't come to hear about money raising, tabernacle building, or any of that. And we don't even know whether it's your vision or God's vision. We don't know how to measure if this vision is authentic. We don't know if there is legitimacy to your claim that God gave you, of all people, a vision. Quite frankly, Rev. Moses, we don't know if you had a vision or a nightmare. All we hear is you running around saying that God told you, 'Build me a sanctuary.'"

On Strategy and Consensus

As I examined the text to better understand Moses' visioning process, I found something terribly wrong. I found something that I believe made it difficult for the people of Israel to accept the authenticity of Moses' vision. Look at the text again:

> And the Lord spake unto Moses, saying, Speak unto the children of Israel, that they bring me an offering: of every man that giveth it willingly with his heart ye shall take my offering. And this is the offering which ye shall take of them; gold, and silver, and brass, and blue, and purple, and scarlet, and fine linen, and goats' hair, and rams' skins dyed red, and badgers' skins, and shittim wood, oil for the light, spices for anointing oil, and for sweet incense, onyx stones, and stones to be set in the ephod, and in the breastplate. And let them make me a sanctuary; that I may dwell among them. (Exod. 25:1–8)

There seem to be at least two things wrong with the vision Moses said God gave to him. First, *Moses had a vision but no strategy.* I don't know much about modern management theory, but I do know that if you have a vision without a strategy, all you really have is an illusion. A vision without a strategy isn't going anywhere. Merely speaking a vision is not enough. At some point, somebody is going to want to know how you're going to make the vision become reality. Vision provides direction, but a strategy is needed to determine how that vision will be carried to completion.

Moses' vision was flawed in a second way: *He had no process for building consensus.* Consensus building is a process by which collective agreement is obtained. Through consensus building, an idea garners support with the hope of gaining approval. It is difficult to achieve a vision unless everyone is given the opportunity to give input on the goals, objectives, and values the vision endorses. Consensus building is necessary to achieve the "buy-in" that is needed before a vision can become viable.

I don't see any process for consensus building in the vision Moses declared. It seems as though Moses could have benefited from management school. He had no committee meetings, visioning sessions, or surveys. He held no board meetings or church meetings. No votes were taken. He was simply a man of God who spoke to the people of God with the word of God on behalf of God, saying, "Let them make me a sanctuary that I may dwell among them."

Despite the apparent flaws in Moses' visioning process, perhaps there are still some godly principles of visionary leadership that require our examination. First, it is clear that Moses was seeking to get the people to see something on the inside that could not be seen on the outside. To achieve this goal, Moses began by listing materials that would be used to construct the tabernacle. Moses sought to have the people mentally and spiritually conceptualize how the tabernacle would look. He had no design plan or superstructure. Nor did he have an architectural rendering of the final product. He simply listed materials.

Moses understood that for the tabernacle to be built, it must first be built on the inside before it is built on the outside. He knew that if the tabernacle didn't first reside in the Israelites' spirits, the ultimate structure wouldn't be of any value. If it wasn't in their hearts, the ultimate structure, no matter how well constructed, would not last long. If the tabernacle was not imprinted in their spiritual center, all the blueprints in the world would be worthless.

God is preparing us to be His sanctuary. He does not dwell in buildings; He dwells in us. If God can build the tabernacle in our spirits, He won't have to worry about the building of a physical tabernacle. I need Him to prepare me to be a sanctuary. I want the tabernacle of God to be in me. As the popular worship chorus says, "Lord, prepare me to be a sanctuary, pure and holy, tried and true."

Some additional principles require our examination. First, Moses' vision could not be seen with the human eye. And it could not be built by human intelligence but by divine initiative alone. When mere humans are the architects and builders in the tabernacle building business, we feel the need to know everything we can. We feel a need to ask questions from morning until night. We feel as though we have every right to healthy skepticism.

On the other hand, when the tabernacle is built by divine initiative, the focus is different. When God is the architect, some questions need not be asked, some answers need not be sought, some issues need not be raised. After all, God is the Chief Architect. He laid the foundations of the earth. "Who hath measured the waters in the hollow of his hand, and meted out heaven with the span, and comprehended the dust of the earth in a measure, and weighed the mountains in scales, and the hills in a balance" (Isa. 40:12).

On Faith and Finance

In trying to understand Moses' visioning process, one final principle is key: In the final analysis, tabernacle building is a matter of faith, not finance. And faith is a matter of who you know, not what you have.

Faith looks at impossibility and says, "If ye have faith as a grain of mustard seed, . . . nothing shall be impossible unto you" (Matt. 17:20).

Faith looks at trouble-makers and says, "Fret not thyself because of evildoers, neither be thou envious against the workers of iniquity. For they shall soon be cut down like the grass, and wither as the green herb" (Ps. 37:1–2).

Faith looks at failure and says, "Nevertheless at thy word I will let down the net" (Luke 5:5).

Faith looks at opposition and says, "Who shall separate us from the love of Christ? shall tribulation, or distress, or persecution, or famine, or nakedness, or peril, or sword? . . . Nay, in all these things we are more than conquerors through him that loved us" (Rom. 8:35, 37).

Habakkuk said, "The just shall live by his faith" (2:4). The writer of Hebrews said, "Now faith is the substance of things hoped for, the evidence of things not seen" (11:1), and "Without faith it is impossible to please [God]" (v. 6).

Trust is linked to faith, therefore vision must always be examined in a framework of trust. The trust issue in Old Testament tabernacle building was not whether Israel trusted Moses but whether Israel trusted God. Here was the issue for Israel: If you trusted God to take you out of Israel when there was famine to find grain in Egypt; if you trusted God to lead you by the hand out of the land of Pharaoh to a promised land of milk and honey; if you trusted God to stand by your side while Pharaoh's army was hot on your trail; if you trusted God to lead you with a cloud by day and fire by night; if you trusted God to bring you out with a "high hand"— that same God is able to see you through now.

And I know God will see *you* through, because He is faithful. We are engaged in more than a history lesson; you see this principle at work in your own life right now. God has a vision for your life. God is getting ready to set up a sanctuary in your life. He is getting ready to build something in your life that you cannot comprehend—a tabernacle of opportunity. God is getting ready to open up new doors and carve out new pathways for you right now. The same God that blessed you before is the same God that will bless you now.

You may not be able to see all that God is doing for you, but He is ready to bless you right now. You may not have His vision, you may not understand His vision, but He is ready to bless you right now. Whatever you do, don't block your blessing! If you trust God, He will bless you.

I trust in God wherever I may be,
Upon the land or on the rolling sea;
For come what may, from day to day,
My heavenly Father watches over me.
He makes the rose an object of His care,

He guides the eagle through the pathless air,
And surely He remembers me;
My heavenly Father watches over me.
I trust in God, I know He cares for me,

On mountain bleak or on the stormy sea.
Though billows roll, He keeps my soul;
My heavenly Father watches over me.

W. C. Martin

The Tabernacle and the Door

A Door No One Can Shut

Exodus 27:14

> The hangings of one side of the gate shall be fifteen cubits: their pillars three, and their sockets three. And on the other side shall be hangings fifteen cubits: their pillars three, and their sockets three. And for the gate of the court shall be an hanging of twenty cubits, of blue, and purple, and scarlet, and the fine twined linen, wrought with needlework: and their pillars shall be four, and their sockets four. (Exod. 27:14–16)

> I am the door: by me if any man enter in, he shall be saved, and shall go in and out, and find pasture. (John 10:9)

God's instructions for constructing the tabernacle were clear but by no means complete. God had specified the materials to be used: gold; silver; brass; blue, purple, and scarlet yarn; fine linen; goat hair; ram skins; badger skins; acacia wood; and more. There was no question that God required a tabernacle to be constructed in the wilderness, and there was no question that He had provided everything Israel would need for the construction process. The only questions that remained were whether the children of Israel could follow God's instructions and whether they had the faith to follow God's vision even when they could not see it. That is why, in this text, God not only described the materials to be used in the construction of the tabernacle, but He also offered a rendering of what the tabernacle would look like in its completed form. Yes, it is clear that the instructions for constructing the tabernacle were clear but by no means complete.

A careful study of the tabernacle building process allows us to understand that our God is a God of precision and detail. He, who sets the timing for seasons and puts whirling constellations in their orbits for eons of time, did not have a haphazard or imprecise process for constructing the tabernacle. These passages contain intricate details about elements of the tabernacle, including the ark, the mercy seat, the cherubim, the table, the dishes, the veil, the curtains, and the golden candlestick.

Let's look at the tabernacle in detail, keeping in mind that the tabernacle was constructed in a way that allowed it to be carried by the Israelites in all their travels. It was never intended to remain in one location; it was a portable sanctuary.

The tabernacle was fifty-five feet long, eighteen feet wide, and eighteen feet high. The wood used to build its furniture was from the acacia tree, a tree whose wood was less subject to decay than any other in the Sinai region. The walls consisted of upright boards set in silver sockets held firm by pillars and connecting bars, all of which were overlaid with gold, thereby giving the appearance that the structure was made of solid gold. The roof was formed by four sets of curtains. The innermost curtains were made of "fine twined linen, and blue, and purple, and scarlet: with cherubims of cunning work" (Exod. 26:1). The tabernacle was sectioned into two parts by a rich and beautiful veil suspended from gold-plated pillars. A similar veil closed the entrance to the first section, or the outer court. The veil was made of beautifully arranged threads of blue, purple, and scarlet. Inlaid with threads of gold and silver were cherubim representing the angelic host of the heavenly sanctuary sent to minister to the people of God on earth.

The intricate details did not end there. There were also gold-plated walls reflecting the light from the golden candlestick, the table of showbread, and the altar of incense glittering with gold. Beyond the second veil was the sacred ark with its cherubim, and above it the holy Shekinah, the visible manifestation of Jehovah's presence. All were but a dim reflection of the glories of the temple of God in heaven, the great center of the work for humankind's redemption.

A Necessary Door

Another essential element of the tabernacle that must be understood before going forward is the door. It seems to be a rather obscure element having little value or obvious meaning, but a person couldn't enter the tabernacle or have an appreciation for its splendor without entering through the door.

> The hangings of one side of the gate shall be fifteen cubits: their pillars three, and their sockets three. And on the other side shall be hangings fifteen cubits: their pillars three, and their sockets three. And for the gate of the court shall be an hanging of twenty cubits, of blue, and purple, and scarlet, and fine twined linen, wrought with needlework: and their pillars shall be four, and their sockets four. (Exod. 27:14–16)

On the surface, this text appears to offer no preaching value. There appears to be no meat on these bones or gravy in this pot! I assure you, however, that a deeper examination will prove otherwise.

Functionally speaking, a door is nothing more than a way in and a way out, a mere opening in a wall, but without which the wall would be an impenetrable barrier. But doors are also symbolic, representing access or an opportunity for movement that may not have existed before. One's relationship to the door determines if one is "in" or "out."

Like it or not, we are citizens of a society that functions and regulates itself by doors. A door may be visible or invisible, and sooner or later you will be forced to deal with the reality of doors. Let's examine some doors that exist in our world.

Every day we live with the reality of *economic doors*. The size of your bank account very often determines the doors that open or shut in your face. The nature of your investments and the size of your portfolio determine where you live and how well you live. If you live among the "haves," what you have can take you where you want to go. On the other hand, if you live among the "have-nots," don't bother to leave home, because you're not going anywhere. If the ship you were waiting on came in with nothing on it, you know about closed doors. But having money opens many doors.

Let's examine another door. Every day we live with the reality of *racial doors*. The fact that we live today in a multicultural, multiethnic society of the twenty-first century may lead some to believe that color and race don't matter anymore. Some believe that Martin Luther King's "dream" has become a reality and that we are no longer judged by the color of our skin but by the content of our character. However, I believe, as philosopher-professor Cornell West does, that race still matters.

Racism has taken on subtler forms, bigotry has put on new garments, but every once in a while something will happen to remind me of who I am and where I've come from. Every once in a while a door will slam in my face and I'll suddenly remember why. Every once in a while somebody will say something about racial profiling, or about redlining African American neighborhoods, or about the incarceration of African American males, and I will be reminded that the struggle is not over. Every once in a while somebody will slip up and say something that's politically incorrect that will remind me that my daddy was right when he said, "I'm going to be black for the rest of my life." Whether you know it or not, black folk still have to deal with racial doors.

Let's look at a third door. Every day we live with the reality of the *church door*. I believe that from time to time the church is guilty of being exclusive. The church can become a society unto itself with admission standards that can keep people in or out. In the house of God, there may be cliques, social sets, in-crowds, and "baptized bourgeoisie." A cultural mind-set develops with regard to who is welcome and who is not. A whole lot of folks are on the "Not Welcome" list. The homeless who don't smell like you are not welcome. Drug users who used in the alley before they came into church this morning are not welcome. Anybody who does not look like us; think like us; drive what we drive; live where we live; or dress, sing, or shout like us is not welcome.

Be careful with the doors of judgment and exclusion. The Bible says you don't need to worry about the speck in somebody else's eye; you need to worry about that two-by-four that's in your own. The only reason any of us is here right now is because of the amazing grace of God. Jesus says, "whosoever will," may come to Him (Rev. 22:17).

Doors are nothing new. Examining this matter of doors serves primarily as a prelude to understanding that during the whole of their history, Israel has had to deal with doors. For 430 years, Israel lived as slaves in a foreign land. Slavery represented a closed door in Israel's history, a barrier through which they could not break. Slavery was the obstacle that could not be overcome, the impregnable wall that could not be scaled or broken through. The exile of slavery created in Israel a psychological door through which they could not escape. Even when Israel thought about a life other than a life of slavery, they would always come face-to-face with the inescapable closed door that Pharaoh represented.

At this point in our text, however, God changed the paradigm:

> And the Lord spake unto Moses, saying, Speak unto the children of Israel, that they bring me an offering: of every man that giveth it willingly with his heart ye shall take my offering.

And this is the offering which ye shall take of them; gold, and silver, and brass, and blue, and purple, and scarlet, and fine linen, and goats' hair. And rams' skins dyed red, and badgers' skins, and shittim wood, oil for the light, spices for anointing oil, and for sweet incense, onyx stones, and stones to be set in the ephod, and in the breastplate. And let them make me a sanctuary; that I may dwell among them. (Exod. 25:1–8)

In the midst of the wilderness, with only the resources they had been able to bring with them from their exile in Egypt, the people were to build a tabernacle. God gave them a detailed list of materials they would need to accomplish their assigned task, as well as comprehensive instructions of how the construction was to proceed.

God instructed that the tabernacle should include the building of a door on the east that would serve as the only entrance into the court and was to be situated in the center of the east fence with fifteen cubits, or twenty-two feet, of court fence on either side. The height of the gate, or door, to the tabernacle was to be seven and a half feet. The width of the door was to be thirty feet. God also specified that the door was to have four colors and was to be held erect with four pillars (Exod. 27:16).

Going In

It is important to understand that the door to the tabernacle represents a picture of Christ. Some biblical exegetes suggest that the four colors and the four pillars are representative of the four Gospels that illuminate the life of Christ to the world. Symbolically, blue speaks of Christ's heavenly nature, purple of His royalty as King of Kings, scarlet of His suffering and blood, and white of His sinlessness.

Now I want to share four things the door symbolizes. First, if the exodus demonstrates God's ability to bring you out, the door of the tabernacle symbolizes God's ability to bring you in. If you find yourself in a tight situation, God is able to take you out of it. When you were down and couldn't get up, when every road was blocked, when every door was shut, when there was no way up and no way out, nobody but the Lord brought you out. Every time Israel looked at that door to the tabernacle, they had to remember that they did not get where they were on their own; God had brought them there.

Similarly, every time you and I pass through the door of the church, the door reminds us that neither you nor I made it this far by ourselves.

God stepped into the middle of your wilderness. God stepped into the midst of your oppressive situation.

God stepped into the middle of whatever enslaved you.

God stepped into the middle of your mess.

God stepped into the middle of whatever it was that was holding you back, keeping you down, or putting a door in your path. No matter how far "out" I may be, it is in the divine intention of God to bring me back in.

I am where I am today because God brought me out and then brought me in.

Out of my slavery into salvation.

Out of my Red Sea into a dry land.

Out of hunger into milk and honey.

Out of indignity into humanity.

Out of dishonor into grace.

Out of oppression into opportunity.

Out of weakness into power.

Out of pain into praise.

Out of defeat into victory.

In the midst of a wilderness, God told Moses, "Let them make me a sanctuary that I may dwell among them." In the process of describing for Israel the building of the tabernacle, God told them to build a gate, or door, to the tabernacle. The door symbolized for the people of Israel that the same God who brought them out of bondage would bring them into the tabernacle.

The second thing the door symbolizes is Israel's ability to break away from their past. When the people of Israel were on their way out of slavery, they literally took with them everything out of Egypt they could beg, borrow, or steal. Exodus 12:36 says, "The LORD gave the people favour in the sight of the Egyptians, so that they lent unto them such things as they required. And they spoiled the Egyptians."

The Israelites borrowed from the Egyptians, and those from whom they could not borrow, they stole from. They had boxes. They had bags. They had fried chicken and collard greens. They had macaroni and cheese. Everything that was not nailed down, they brought with them on their march to the Promised Land.

But then God instructed Israel to build a tabernacle with a door in the middle of the east wall. And Israel could not bring anything into the tabernacle that they had brought out of Egypt. When they entered the tabernacle, the only thing they were to bring was an animal as an offering of sacrifice to die in their place. When the worshiper brought the animal, he would lay his hands on the head of the animal and confess his sins, thus transferring his sin to the animal (Lev. 1:4). Then the animal, which was not guilty of his own sin but that of someone else, was killed. The priest then caught the blood and carried it to the brazen altar, where he sprinkled some on the four horns and poured the remainder at the base of the altar.

Just as the door reminds us of Israel's entrance process, it also reminds us that when we come to worship, there are some things we don't need to bring in with us. If Israel could break away from their past, then surely you can break away from yours. Leave any baggage that you've been carrying at the door. And leave behind that guilt you've been carrying for so long. When you walk through the door, the door means: Whatever was yesterday, was yesterday; whatever was in your past, let it be in your past. Whatever memory you have, let it be a memory. Whatever you used to be you don't have to be anymore. You don't have to bring your bags, you don't have to wash your linen, you don't have to tell all your business, and you don't have to open up your garbage. It's over! Get over it!

If you want to break away from your past, just walk through the door. The door says you can start over again. The door says you can have another chance. The door says forgiveness is possible. The door says grace is guaranteed. The door says God still looks beyond your fault and sees your need. Walking through the door allows you to break from your past.

The third thing God shows through the tabernacle door is that even in a desperate situation, there is a way into God's presence. I cannot think of a more desperate circumstance than the one in which Israel found themselves. Yet God provided a tabernacle. In that tabernacle, God provided a door on the east side. By providing that door, God was indicating that it's not just any door—it's God's door. God said that when you come through that door, it's a door made by His design and specifications. When you come through that door, you can expect something to happen, for you will be standing in the presence of the almighty God. To come through this door is to stand in the presence of:

Jehovah-Yahweh—the self-existent one

Jehovah-Jireh—God the provider

Jehovah-Nissi—Yahweh is my banner

Jehovah-Shalom—Yahweh is my peace

Jehovah-Sabbaoth—Yahweh of hosts

Jehovah-Maccaddeshem—Yahweh your sanctifier

Jehovah-Raah—Yahweh is my shepherd

Jehovah-Tsidkenu—Yahweh our righteousness

Jehovah-Shammah—Yahweh who is present

Jehovah-Rapha—Yahweh who heals

Jehovah-Elohim—Yahweh, the mighty one

When you come in this door, you stand in the presence of Adonai, Elohim, El Elyon, El Roi, El Shaddai, El Olam, El Elohe Israel, Yeshua, Christos, Kurios, Soter, and Theos.

On a Sabbath morning, I come to stand in God's presence. I come to glory in the awesomeness of God and to magnify His name. I say with David: "I will bless the LORD at all times: his praise shall continually be in my mouth. My soul shall make her boast in the LORD: the humble shall hear thereof, and be glad. O magnify the LORD with me, and let us exalt his name together" (Ps. 34:1–3).

The door symbolizes a fourth and final reality. After I have gone through my wilderness situation, when my vision is blurred and I do not see what God sees, when I am challenged to build a tabernacle I do not understand, God brings me out, brings me in, gets rid of my baggage, and lets me stand in His presence. Then, when I am standing in His presence, I understand that the door is the ultimate symbol of liberation.

Understand that this liberation means more than freedom. Israel was free when they walked out of Egypt and made it across the Red Sea. Israel was free the moment they declared, "We'll never turn back no more." But Israel was only truly liberated when they walked through the door.

Entering the doors of the church should also liberate us. After all God went through to get you here, when you get here, you ought to be able to do what you want. You ought to be able to praise like you want to praise. You ought to be able to shout like you want to shout. When I come to church, I don't want to have to act like somebody wants me to act. I've been doing what other people want me to do all week long. Every time I come into God's house, a spirit of liberty falls on me. Paul said: "Where the Spirit of the Lord is, there is liberty" (2 Cor. 3:17).

If I want to cry, let me cry.

If I want to run, let me run.

If I want to shout, let me shout.

If you don't like how I shout, then get out of my way.

When I come through this door, the only thing I can tell you is, "You don't know what the Lord done for me!"

I don't know what they sang in that tabernacle, but when they walked through the door, I heard somebody sing:

> *I'm free, praise the Lord, I'm free.*
> *No longer bound, no more chains holding me.*
> *I'm just confessing, it's just a blessing,*
> *Praise the Lord, hallelujah, I'm free.*

The Tabernacle and the Fire

Let the Fire Burn!

Exodus 27:1

And thou shalt make an altar of shittim wood, five cubits long, and five cubits broad; the altar shall be foursquare: and the height thereof shall be three cubits. . . . And thou shalt make his pans to receive his ashes, and his shovels, and his basins, and his fleshhooks, and his firepans: all the vessels thereof thou shalt make of brass. (Exod. 27:1, 3)

And the fire upon the altar shall be burning in it; it shall not be put out: and the priest shall burn wood on it every morning, and lay the burnt offering in order upon it; and he shall burn thereon the fat of the peace offerings. The fire shall ever be burning upon the altar; it shall never go out. (Lev. 6:12–13)

The first five books of the Old Testament, the Pentateuch, tell the story of the relationship between a brokenhearted God and sinful humans. Somewhere in a crescent we call Fertile and in a garden we call Eden, God began to respond to incredible sin with an incredible love.

You know the story in the book of Genesis, the story of a God who formed man with His own hands. You know the story of a God who breathed into man's nostrils the breath of life. You know the story of a God who provided a garden with fruit and flowers of every description, the story of a God who gave to man everything he needed.

God gave man dominion over the fish of the sea and the fowl of the air. God gave man every herb-bearing seed and every tree-yielding seed. God gave man a woman to be his companion and helper and said to them, "Be fruitful and multiply." God said, "You can have it all. You have dominion over everything you see from the east to the west, from the north to the south. Everything I have is yours. I have only one stipulation: Don't eat from the tree of the knowledge of good and evil." You know the rest of the saga of Eve and the serpent, of temptation's power, and of innocence and paradise lost.

After humankind sinned and fell from God's grace, the God-human relationship was never the same. Because of sin, the divine contract entered into in Eden was made null and void. That is why the Pentateuch tells the story of the relationship between a brokenhearted God and sinful man.

God's response to humankind's disobedience could have been merely punitive, but it was not. Although God banished Adam and Eve from the garden, the glory of this story is that despite their sin, He persistently pursued humankind. This God who had been affronted was ever in search of an instrument of reconciliation. This God whose eyes were forever cast on a reprobate and unrepentant creation stood in the vortex of human history with a word of forgiveness on His lips and restoration in His heart. This God who sorrowfully sensed the awful work of sin was forever determined to make amazing grace available to humankind.

It seems strange that He who made the covenant and did not break it nevertheless sought to reestablish it. It seems peculiar that He who wrote the contract and kept it was forever in search of the one who broke it. Amazingly, God was determined to repair the breach, heal the wound, overcome the separation, close the chasm, renew the contract, and settle the account.

This God of the Genesis narrative repeatedly made covenants. First with Adam, then with Noah, Abraham, Moses, and David. Over and over again, the covenant was broken. So greatly was the covenant broken that the prophet Jeremiah accused Israel of an endemic wickedness, of being a degenerate plant, backsliding, and playing the harlot under every green tree (Jer. 2:19–20). So greatly was the covenant broken that when all the charges had been brought against the nation, Isaiah, wanting to convene a court of Eternity, cried out to Israel, "Come now, and let us reason together, . . . though your sins be as scarlet, they shall be as white as snow; though they be red like crimson, they shall be as wool" (Isa. 1:18).

This God of the Genesis narrative who with sorrow in His eyes banished man from the garden is the same God who placed a flaming sword at the east end of the garden to point the way home for wayward humankind (Gen. 3:24). This God of Genesis is the same God of John's Revelation who with hopeful expectancy declared from the far reaches of heaven, "Behold, I stand at the door, and knock: if any man hear my voice, and open the door, I will come in to him, and will sup with him, and he with me" (Rev. 3:20).

This is an amazing story of how God continued to love, pursue, and reconcile humankind to himself in spite of their persistent disobedience and defiance. It continues in the book of Exodus during the wilderness wanderings of the children of Israel. There you will find that in the midst of their sin, in the midst of God's liberating them from their long night of bondage and oppression, in the midst of their incredible journey from a land of slavery to a land of freedom, God spoke these words to Moses: "Speak unto the children of Israel, that they bring me an offering: of every man that giveth it willingly with his heart ye shall take my offering. . . . And let them make me a sanctuary; that I may dwell among them" (Exod. 25:2, 8).

First-Class Construction

God didn't just want any old tabernacle. God gave very precise specifications for how this portable sanctuary was to be built and described the quality of construction materials required. Everything about the tabernacle was to be first class and five star.

You can be sure that when God built His church, there was nothing cheap or chintzy about it. God used the finest wood and gold, bronze, and silver. He was so meticulous that no detail was left to chance or debate. God specified the reason the tabernacle should be built: "that I may dwell among them." His vision for the tabernacle was one that human eyes very often cannot see and human minds cannot comprehend.

Exodus 27:1–2 explains the building of the brazen altar:

> And thou shalt make an altar of shittim wood, five cubits long, and five cubits broad; the altar shall be foursquare: and the height thereof shall be three cubits. And thou shalt make the horns of it upon the four corners thereof: his horns shall be of the same: and thou shalt overlay it with brass. And thou shalt make his pans to receive his ashes, and his shovels, and his basons, and his fleshhooks, and his firepans: all the vessels thereof thou shalt make of brass.

Consider the brazen altar. The Hebrew word for the brazen altar, *mizbēah,* literally means "slaughter place." The brazen altar was situated in the tabernacle courtyard and was constructed of acacia wood and built off the ground. It was accessible throughout the day for people to come and offer their sacrifices.

When offering a sacrifice at the brazen altar, an Israelite would bring an animal to die in his place. He would lay his hands on the head of the animal and confess his sins, thereby transferring his sin to the animal. Then the animal, which was not burdened with its own sin but that of someone else, was killed. After the animal was killed, the priest would catch the blood and carry it to the brazen altar. There he would sprinkle drops of blood on the four horns, or projections, on the corners of the altar and would pour the rest at its base.

There were five accessories on the altar, all of which were made of brass and copper: the pans, which were used to carry out the ashes; the shovels, which were used for picking up the ashes and tending the fire; the basins, which held the blood of the sacrificial animal; the fleshhooks, which were used for keeping the sacrifice in the middle of the fire so it could be totally consumed; and the firepans, which were used to carry fire from the brazen altar to the altar of incense in the Holy of Holies.

The fire that was brought before the Lord's presence could only be taken from the gold-covered altar of incense. It is important to understand the significance of both the sacrifice that was placed on the altar and the fire that burned on the altar. Look first at the sacrifice.

Bringing God Your Best

Sacrifice has several implications. First, for Israel, sacrifice signified a *costly religion*. When people came to offer sacrifices, they did not bring the worst they had, they brought the best. They brought the finest of the flock, a lamb that had neither spot nor blemish. Whatever they brought for the sacrifice cost them something. They did not approach the altar to give little; they approached it to give as much as they possibly could. There is something wrong with a religion that does not cost anything.

But sacrifice is more than a matter of cost. The children of Israel also took seriously their obligation to God. Their sacrifice, then, signified a serious religion. When Israel built the tabernacle, they built it with the architectural splendor that God required. They used the finest materials available. When they arrived at the temple, they went through the fence and then through the door. Once they got through the door, they stood face-to-face with the altar of sacrifice, where the first thing they saw was the blood.

Like Israel, the first thing we ought to look for when we enter into the house of the Lord should be something serious. You shouldn't look for your friends or check to see which choir is singing or which preacher is preaching. Don't look to see if your name is on the program. Don't even look at the program. When you enter the house of the Lord, you need to look for something serious.

You ought to look for something that reminds you that the only reason you are there is because Jesus' blood has been shed. That's serious.

You ought to look for something that reminds you that somebody died so that you might live. That's serious.

You need to look for something that reminds you that you were born in sin and shaped in iniquity; something that reminds you that your sin is ever before you; something that reminds you that the reason you are in God's house is not because you're holy, and not because you're righteous, and not because you're free from sin, but because you need to stand before the Almighty to repent of your sin. That's serious.

When the children of Israel came to the tabernacle, the first thing they saw was the place of sacrifice, a symbol of the seriousness of their religion.

Third, sacrifice on the brazen altar symbolized *authentic worship*. We know that the children of Israel brought animals with them to the tabernacle to be sacrificed and that sacrifice was the first order of business in worship. Worship was not really worship unless the act of sacrifice took place.

The story of Abraham and Isaac, found in Genesis 22, will help this concept come alive for you: "And it came to pass after these things, that God did tempt Abraham, and said unto him, Abraham: and he said, Behold, here I am. And he said, Take now thy son, thine only son Isaac, whom thou lovest, and get thee into the land of Moriah; and offer him there for a burnt offering upon one of the mountains which I will tell thee of" (vv. 1–2).

Understand what was happening here. Abraham was more than a hundred years old, and Isaac was the son he had been waiting for all his life. Yet God ordered Abraham to take his only son to the altar of sacrifice. It seemed impossible that Abraham would have another son. Hagar was gone. Sarah was somewhere saying, "Don't look at me. I'm done!" Nothing could have been more costly or serious to Abraham and Sarah than the sacrifice of their son.

The significance of this story lies in Genesis 22:5, which says, "Abraham said unto his young men, Abide ye here with the ass; and I and the lad will go yonder and worship, and come again to you." Abraham understood that his sacrifice was an act of worship. You cannot worship God unless you bring something with you. More than that, whatever you bring ought to cost you something. It is only when you bring something to the experience of worship that costs you something that God knows you're serious.

My worship is not just about my singing, praying, or occupying the same pew every Sunday. My worship is about bringing something to God that is so pivotal to my being that when I give it up, I don't know how I'm going to make it. I must give God my all. When I think about the sacrifice that God has made for me, giving God my best isn't hard to do. When I think about what God had to go through to get me where I am, when I couldn't do anything for myself, I refuse to give God leftovers. I'm going to give Him the best I have.

Sacrifice is significant in one more way. Sacrifice symbolizes *the blessing you need* when you need it. Let's delve a little deeper into Abraham's story. God told Abraham to take Isaac to the altar of sacrifice. Abraham was so caught up in the worship experience that he was willing to give God his only son. Yet as soon as Abraham put Isaac on the wood and, with tears in his eyes, stretched him out, picked up the knife, and prepared to slit his throat, God provided a ram in a bush. That ram was just what Abraham needed when he needed it.

God will give you what you need when you need it. God always has a ram in the bush. The act of sacrifice activates your blessing.

As soon as you act with seriousness, God puts angels into action.

As soon as you act in obedience to God's Word, God sends ambassadors to come to your aid.

As soon as you step out by faith, God sends legions to your rescue.

When you look back over your life, you'll see that God has been putting rams in your bush for a long time. God has been putting blessings in your path just when you need them most.

God is always by your side, just when you need Him most.

He always makes a way out of no way, just when you need Him most.

When you don't have a dime, He gives you full measure, pressed down, shaken together, and running over, just when you need it most.

When you can't pay your bills, you've seen Him open the windows of heaven and pour you out a blessing, just when you need it most.

And when everything else in your life is running late, He is always on time. The old folk were right when they used to say, "He may not come when you want Him, but He's always right on time!"

That's why bringing a sacrifice is an important part of worship. Even though you are not required to bring any lambs and goats, you must willingly bring something with you when you come to worship. As much as God has done for you, nobody should ever have to beg you to put something in the offering plate. As many scrapes and scraps as the Lord has brought you through, nobody should have to beg you to build the tabernacle. As many times as the Lord has given you more than you ever expected and more than you ever deserved, nobody should ever have to beg you to bring your tithes and offerings.

Don't think that merely bringing "things" to God constitutes a sufficient sacrifice. God doesn't want things; the real sacrifice God wants is you. God didn't really want Isaac; He wanted Abraham. God didn't want the goats and sheep that the children of Israel laid on the altar; God wanted them. God wants you too! Paul said it best: "I beseech you therefore, brethren, by the mercies of God, that ye present your bodies a living sacrifice, holy, acceptable unto God, which is your reasonable service" (Rom. 12:1).

The Purpose of Fire

Yet there is more than sacrifice; there is fire. Look at the role that the fire played in the sacrificial process. Five accessories were used at the altar, one of which was a firepan used to carry the fire from the brazen altar to the altar of incense in the Holy of Holies. Carrying the fire to the altar of incense was the final step in the act of sacrifice. The process of sacrifice was never complete without the presence of fire.

Fire was needed in the tabernacle for three reasons. First, fire served as God's *cleansing agent.* In authentic worship, God's power is there to cleanse. When I sacrifice my life before the altar, God's presence cleanses me. His grace purifies me. When I come in stained by the filth of the world, I need God to clean me up on the inside and then clean me up on the outside. His holy fire cleanses.

The second reason fire was needed in the tabernacle was that it symbolized *uncontainable energy.* Fire is distinctive in that it has the capacity to burn everywhere it goes. On the day of Pentecost, the church caught on fire spiritually when the Holy Spirit descended. Fire has so much energy that when combustion takes place it doesn't set just one thing on fire, it sets everything around it on fire.

When you come to worship with your sacrifice, and as a result of that sacrifice you get blessed, a little fire starts in you. Sometimes you try to hold on to your fire. In fact, you may even try to pretend you don't have any fire. But sooner or later, the fire begins to burn and you just can't keep it to yourself. Once you start burning, you can't help but set ablaze everything you touch. Before you know it, your fire lights my fire, and my fire lights somebody else's. And soon the whole place is on fire. Fire was needed in the tabernacle because of its uncontainable energy.

The third and final reason for the presence of the fire in the tabernacle is that it represented the *continuing presence of God.*

> And the Lord spake unto Moses, saying, Command Aaron and his sons, saying, This is the law of the burnt offering: It is the burnt offering, because of the burning upon the altar all night unto the morning, and the fire of the altar shall be burning in it. . . . it shall not be put out: and the priest shall burn wood on it every morning, and lay the burnt offering in order upon it; and he shall burn thereon the fat of the peace offerings. The fire shall ever be burning upon the altar; it shall never go out. (Lev. 6:8–9, 12–13)

The ever-burning fire on the altar was a sign to the children of Israel so that whenever they came through the gate, or door, they would know that God was present. And when I go to church, I too want to know, even symbolically, that God is present. I don't want to come to church if the fire is out. After all I've been catching all week long, when I go into the house of the Lord, I want to know that the fire is still burning. I want to know God is present. When I walk through the door, something on the inside of me will know God is alive, active, and available in my life.

It was the priest's role to assure that the fire was always burning. No self-respecting priest would ever let the fire go out. So, as the priest of this tabernacle, I've decided that no matter what, we ought to let the fire burn.

If nobody else is present, let the fire burn.

If nobody else shows up, as long as God is in this place, let the fire burn.

If the deacons don't show up, let the fire burn.

If the choir doesn't sing, let the fire burn.

If the preacher won't preach, let the fire burn.

Somebody needs to feel the fire burning. Somebody's home is in trouble. Let the fire burn.

Somebody's marriage is about to break up. Somebody's child is strung out on drugs. Somebody whose heart is broken in a thousand pieces needs to stand in the assuring presence of God. Let the fire burn.

Women and children have been battered and bruised. Let the fire burn. Men's dignity and self-esteem have been destroyed. Let the fire burn.

Folks dressed up on the outside are hurting like hell on the inside. Let the fire burn.

Repairing the Breach

The Old Testament tells the story of the relationship between a brokenhearted and loving God with sinful covenant-breaking man. In order to repair the breach, to heal the wound, to overcome the separation, to close the chasm and restore the relationship, sacrifice had to be made. The sacrifice of bulls and goats was not enough, yet a blood sacrifice had to be made, because without the shedding of blood there could be no remission of sin.

And because the sacrifice of bulls and goats could not atone for humankind's sin, a council was called in the throne room of God to find someone who could leave heaven and go to earth to atone for humankind's sin. Who could provide the sacrifice that man needed and God required? Names were called to see who was qualified for such a task.

Noah couldn't go because he was somewhere drunk.

Abraham couldn't go because he was known to be a liar.

Moses couldn't go because he still had blood on his hands.

Jacob couldn't go because he was known as a deceiver and a cheat.

David couldn't go because he still had Bathsheba's perfume on his sheets.

Job couldn't go because he still had sores from the crown of his head to the soles of his feet.

Samson couldn't go because he had a fresh haircut.

Jonah couldn't go because he was still in the belly of a great fish.

Isaiah couldn't go because he was caught up with King Uzziah.

Jeremiah couldn't go because they couldn't count on the reliability of a crybaby.

The angel Michael couldn't go because they said he was too slow.

The angel Gabriel couldn't go because he was somewhere on the outskirts of heaven blowing his horn.

But about that time there was a stirring at the right hand of God the Father. Jesus stepped in and said, "I'll go." And He went down from heaven to earth. He went down in His divinity but arrived in His humanity.

Many don't understand all the fuss about Jesus because He was just a common man.

He came to earth as a common baby.

He was delivered to a virgin in a common stable.

He was birthed in a common village.

He was wrapped in common clothes.

He was placed in a common manger.

He was reared as a common carpenter, and the common people heard Him gladly.

He drank wine with common sinners.

He preached from a common boat.

He rode on a common mule.

He washed common feet.

He broke common bread.

He was tried for a common crime.

He was treated like a common thief.

He became a common lamb.

He was crucified on a common tree.

He was pierced with a common spear and hung up on common nails.

He died a common death.

He was placed in a common grave.

On the third day, Jesus arose from the dead. But there was nothing common about that. Early on Easter Sunday morning, He got up with all power in His hand. He is the Lamb of God who takes away the sin of the world. Jesus is the perfect sacrifice.

> *Your only Son, no sin to hide,*
> *But You have sent Him from Your side*
> *To walk upon this guilty sod,*
> *And to become the Lamb of God.*
>
> Twila Paris

Do You See What I See?

I could have been wrong. It may be that I did not give the conflict in our community deep-enough prayer and reflection. The problems that surface in communities that affect large institutions may not always be issues that are merely black and white. The conflict we faced certainly had a racial subtext; it is clear that in every circumstance of gentrification, race is always an issue. The issues are most likely those that are occasioned by shifting populations and changing lifestyles.

Those whom we consider our enemies often are not—they simply reflect new and different ways of thinking and behaving. The values the church holds are different from the values of our postmodern culture. There is no way to avoid that difference.

It is particularly important, however, for those of us in the Christian community to be open to visions and voices that are not necessarily our own and to struggle until every avenue of communication has been exhausted. Communication—both internal and external—is the key to life both for the church and for the community it serves.

The tragedy of our situation was that our new neighbors failed to see the church's role in becoming a part of a community and not merely running roughshod over the institutions and persons who for decades of time have created and defined the neighborhood it now seeks to join. Regrettably, both the church and the community lost the opportunity for genuine dialogue and conversation.

I am confident that we arrived at the appropriate decision in terms of the future growth and stability of the church. In the process, because of things I could neither sense nor see, I may have lost the opportunity to really talk to people who could have become friends and, in so doing, be participating in generating a new and stronger community.

PREACHING
the VISION

PART III

A Visit to the Pastor's Office

She came to my office in the early spring. Her gait was assured, her speech confident. I had no idea what was on her mind, so I was surprised to hear her say, "Pastor, I want to discuss your sermons." As if on cue, my chest swelled with pride, since I was sure that if our conversation was not to be about theology or consist of a discussion on the finer points of biblical interpretation, we were sure to engage in some complimentary dialogue confirming my preaching prowess.

I have learned across the years, however, that the longer one stays in a pastorate, the more comfortable parishioners become. This does not portend any disrespect, mind you, only a wholesome relationship that permits the pew to speak directly to the pulpit. Consequently, her conversation was straightforward. She told me that she had heard as much about the tabernacle as a soul could stand. It was clear to her, she said, that I was about the business of using Scripture as a means toward justifying a building program, the idea of which was singularly my own. Moreover, she informed me that she was not alone in her opinion. She continued, hardly taking a breath, that the theme of my sermons had become the source of conversation on the sidewalk before the service began. The constant diet of building and the incessant "pitch" for money had to come to an end and wasn't I tired of hearing myself preach the same sermon week after week?

I recall sitting in a state of shock and hearing myself speak the words of explanation and justification. I spoke of "calling," of my understanding of God's intention for this ministry, and of my purpose to interpret the vision of God so that the congregation would understand our direction. I instructed the woman that the sermons were intentionally repetitive, a strategy to ensure that the congregation would see the thread of biblical and relevant instruction running through them all. I remember the words that came from my mouth—something to the effect that God's Word is not designed to comfort but to confront. God's Word, said I, is preached not so that we should remain the same, but so that we should be changed. I shudder when I remember that I counseled this confrontational parishioner that "God does not give visions to a committee but to a person, chosen as His vessel to speak the word for a particular house in a particular season. Amen."

As I listened to myself, I wondered if I could believe myself. I wondered if I had resorted to the standard, expected, and often cheap jargon of the craft that was more self-protective than honestly responsive. I wondered if I had really heard what she was saying or if my responses, if not satisfactory, were at least genuine and authentic. I wondered if I had helped her to see the legitimacy of how I handled the preaching craft or if, regrettably, I had sent her back to the pew as disturbed and opposed to my preaching methodology as she was when she first came to call.

As I think back upon that conversation, I am stunned by the realization that the greatest opposition to vision is not vocal but silent. There are few persons with the courage to confront the pastor as this young woman did. We can never know how many sit in silence, preferring that their objections be manifest by their inaction, by their failure to participate financially, and ultimately by a change of fellowship to another congregation. It is even possible to take a vote on the vision and win . . . and still lose. Votes are never an accurate barometer of the acceptance of vision.

Looking back upon that hour, I am convinced that in my own mind and in my own spirit I was trying to convey the right message but perhaps in the wrong manner. I have no doubts that it is through the preaching medium that the people of God come to understand God's purpose and will for their lives and for the church. The Bible is the instructional word of God that is designed to bring light and life to those who will hear.

The more I reflect upon my experience as both pastor and preacher, I am continually awed by the enormity of the task. As I think upon it, it is the nature of this calling to speak words that will not be heard or understood. It is the inescapable nature of this calling to lead people who would rather be left as they are, to guide persons who are content where they are. And for the glory of this calling, Jeremiah landed in a pit, Ezekiel wound up in a graveyard, Isaiah was stuffed into a tree, Peter was crucified upside down, and still other disciples were boiled in oil. This is, indeed, a perilous calling.

Preaching the vision is no walk in the park. Isaiah suggests that those who preach have "beautiful feet" (see Isaiah 52:7). This is an engaging metaphor indeed. If, to follow Isaiah's logic, we only bring good news, speak words of peace, and declare that all is well, we may well have beautiful feet. For those who struggle in this calling, however, even if the feet are beautiful, the shoes are worn. Worn are the sandals that tread over treacherous terrain. Worn are the sandals of those who stand with uneven footing and who must preach in unwelcoming pulpits. Where there is a preacher who straps on preaching shoes and who dares to stand behind a sacred desk, he will stand on feet that are scraped and scarred by a culture and by a church that will not readily receive his word.

The Lexus automobile brand uses as one of its slogans "the relentless pursuit of perfection." Of course, as a marketing strategy the meaning of the message is clear. The relentless pursuit of perfection is on our behalf. We gain the benefit because of their insistence that anything less than perfection would be unacceptable. In large measure, authentic preaching is a relentless pursuit—a pursuit of the vision God has for God's people. Preaching as relentless pursuit is what God has in mind: a relentless pursuit of persons who have been perfected, a relentless pursuit of the organic church that can become the perfected kingdom of God.

Paul's counsel to young Timothy was to "preach the word; be instant in season, out of season" (2 Tim. 4:2). The message: preaching must be relentless. Preaching must be continuous, persistent, unyielding, never failing, never fearing. God has a vision for the future church that is to be preferred over its past. If we have been assigned to the task of proclaiming that vision, we must do so relentlessly! The task of the preacher is not to assure the end, but to endure unto the end. Preach the word . . . relentlessly!

The Tabernacle and the Candlestick

This Little Light of Mine

Exodus 25:31

And thou shalt make a candlestick of pure gold: of beaten work shall the candlestick be made: his shaft, and his branches, his bowls, his knops, and his flowers, shall be of the same. And six branches shall come out of the sides of it; three branches of the candlestick out of the one side, and three branches of the candlestick out of the other side. And in the candlestick shall be four bowls made like unto almonds with their knops and their flowers. (Exod. 25:31–32, 34)

Within sacred Scripture, there is an unmistakable quest for the presence of light as opposed to darkness. One has only to open the Bible to discover that the God of creation is also the God of light. Indeed, the God who called the world into being did so when "the earth was without form, and void; and darkness was upon the face of the deep" (Gen. 1:2). And that's when God said, "Let there be light: and there was light" (v. 3).

In a world of darkness, God brought light. In a world that was clothed in the garments of dark shadows and gloom, God brought light. In a world in which it appeared that people were no longer able to find their way, God stepped into dismal darkness and brought light. In a world in which there were no constellations, no guiding star in the north, no silvery moon to illuminate the night sky, God said, "There must be light." Into this world of swirling midnights and pitch-black cypress swamps, God said, "Let there be light."

Whether in the physical or the psychological realm, without light one cannot see. Absent sight, a person is unable to have a vision for himself or herself. An individual with no vision is on the way to personal destruction. Likewise, if we have no collective vision, *we* are on *our* way to destruction. Proverbs 29:18 is correct: "Where there is no vision, the people perish."

Without light or vision, not only are we individually or collectively headed for destruction, we are also unaware of the possibilities that lie ahead. Put another way, if we live in darkness and have become comfortable with the reality of that darkness, and if we believe that darkness is normative and that any attempt to change the darkness in which we live will be resisted and opposed, we will miss open doors and whatever blessings may have been in our path. If there is no light, we will continue to live with what Howard Thurman called "errors of the mind which make for bad judgment when things seem to be distorted, twisted and misshapen."[1] It is in the darkness that great suffering exists. It is in the darkness that men and women stand helpless in the presence of their own suffering, anguish, and needs, which they cannot meet because they are walking in the dark.

If we have no light and no vision, we will continue to stumble and curse in the darkness. No one will need to put stumbling blocks in our paths, because everything we encounter will be a stumbling block. Without an individual or collective sense of vision, not only is destruction inevitable, not only will we miss opportunities and experience great stumbling blocks, but we also will not recognize if and when God shows up in our circumstance because we will have no appreciation for His presence. And that is why God thought it best, on the morning of creation, to step out on the platform of nothing, speak into nothing, speak *ex nihilo,* or out of nothing, and declare to the universe, "Let there be light!"

Considering Light

The concepts of vision and light can be found in both the Old and New Testaments. Consider light and vision in the Old Testament. From his ash pile, Job suggested that there was something wrong with his eyesight and that even perhaps God participated in his blindness. Said Job: "He hideth himself . . . that I cannot see him." (Job 23:9).

David had been in enough deep valleys and narrow places to know not only the necessity of both light and sight, but also its source. "The LORD is my light and my salvation; whom shall I fear?" (Ps. 27:1). David had also discovered that God's "word is a lamp unto my feet, and a light unto my path" (Ps. 119:105).

Consider light in the New Testament. Everywhere you turn, you see that Jesus was concerned about light and sight. He had an encounter with a beggar named Bartimaeus who cried out, "Jesus, thou Son of David, have mercy on me" (Mark 10:47). And He healed him. One day Jesus met a man who had been born blind. He opened up an ophthalmology clinic on the sidewalk. He mixed up some saliva and dirt and told the man to go and wash in a pool called Siloam. And He healed him (John 9:1–7). When asked about this matter of light and sight, Jesus explained His interest in the subject this way, "If the blind lead the blind, both shall fall into the ditch" (Matt. 15:14).

Indeed, so concerned was Jesus about those who live in the chasm of darkness that He defined His ministry by saying, "The spirit of the Lord is upon me, because he hath anointed me to preach the gospel to the poor; he hath sent me to heal the broken-hearted, to preach deliverance to the captives, and recovering of sight to the blind" (Luke 4:18).

Considering Candlesticks

In the book of Exodus, when the wilderness-wandering Israelites were in desperate midnight circumstances, God gave their leader, Moses, instructions for building a portable tabernacle and its furnishings. Among the other furnishings, such as the ark of the covenant, the brazen altar, the altar of incense, and the table of showbread, God included plans for a furnishing that would provide light: "And thou shalt make a candlestick of pure gold: of beaten work shall the candlestick be made: his shaft, and his branches, his bowls, his knops, and his flowers, shall be of the same. And six branches shall come out of the sides of it; three branches of the candlestick out of the one side, and three branches of the candlestick out of the other side" (Exod. 25:31–32). Since the tabernacle was completely closed in and shut off from light by curtains around it and coverings above it, there was no natural light. Thus, the lampstand was a necessity.

The candlestick, or lampstand (NIV), was to be made of solid gold with a central shaft holding six branches. Note that this stand was not made to hold candles, but lamps that burned oil. It was estimated to be three and a half feet high and two feet wide. By today's gold standard, its value has been estimated at more than $5 million.

Significantly, the Old Testament lampstand is mirrored in the New Testament. In the opening of the book of Revelation, John records that one of the first things he saw in his vision of heaven was lampstands: "I turned to see the voice that spake with me. And being turned, I saw seven golden candlesticks; and in the midst of the seven candlesticks one like unto the Son of man" (Rev. 1:12–13). It becomes clear in Jesus' letter to the church at Ephesus that the candlestick, or lampstand, is the church:

> Unto the angel of the church of Ephesus write; These things saith he that holdeth the seven stars in his right hand, who walketh in the midst of the seven golden candlesticks; Nevertheless I have somewhat against thee, because thou hast left

thy first love. Remember therefore from whence thou art fallen, and repent, and do the first works; or else I will come unto thee quickly, and will remove thy candlestick out of his place, except thou repent. (Rev. 2:1, 4–5)

God had a word of judgment for the church at Ephesus even though they were a hardworking church. They did have programs and ministries. And they kept themselves from false doctrines and false prophets. According to John, they were a church that had labored and not fainted. In a manner of speaking, they were the church that would not quit. Nevertheless, the church that looked so good on the outside had something wrong on the inside. They had forsaken their first love. They knew how to be pious but had lost their passion. They knew how to talk "Christianese" but had forgotten how to praise the God they served. They looked like a church of light but were in fact walking in darkness. They looked good on paper and when sitting in the pew. They looked good in the financial report and when dressed up on Sunday morning. But God was not pleased with their hearts.

If the church is the lampstand, it is responsible for facilitating illumination. If it cannot do so, it lives in darkness and has no vision. Whenever the church finds itself without light, without vision, it loses its right to be called a church and its lampstand is removed.

The Lord's instructions in Exodus 25:31 were, "And thou shalt make a candlestick of pure gold." God wanted a candlestick, or lampstand, of pure gold. Understand that the stick, or stand, does not contain light but is the instrument that displays the light. It is a platform for the lamp. This distinction is significant, because candles and lamps function quite differently. A candle burns by consuming itself. Once a candle is lit, it will begin to burn itself out. A lamp, on the other hand, burns by consuming a continuous supply of oil from another source. God doesn't need candles; God needs lamps.

God knew that Israel needed to rely on an independent continuous source of oil that only the lamp could provide. Leviticus 24:1, 4 says: "And the LORD spake unto Moses, saying, Command the children of Israel, that they bring unto thee pure olive oil beaten for the light, to cause the lamps to burn continually. He shall order the lamps upon the pure candlestick before the LORD continually."

Recognizing the purpose of the lampstand is important. The lampstand held the lamp so that the priests could minister in the tabernacle. It allowed the priest to be seen by the worshipers as they came through the door.

Let me say that again. The purpose of the lampstand was to hold the lamp so that *someone* could be seen when worshipers came through the door. The lampstand's purpose was to hold the lamp so that those who had just dropped their baggage at the door would be able to see light when they came through the door. Its purpose was to hold the lamp so that those who had just struggled to get out of a land of darkness, those who had just dropped everything at the door, and those who had laid their sacrifice on the altar would be able to focus their attention on the reason they came to worship in the first place, knowing that they were standing in the very presence of the living God.

Each lamp was connected to a central branch in the middle of the lampstand. The priest's task was to maintain the oil in the lamp so that the lamp would never go out. The source of this oil was the olive tree.

Just outside the city of Jerusalem is a garden situated on a mountain called the Mount of Olives. Jesus was found there one night praying until "sweat like drops of blood came down." He was taken from the Mount of Olives and beaten all night long. When they beat Him, He became the Olive Tree for you and me. In the same manner that the olive oil is the source of light for the lampstand, Jesus is the continuous source of light for the world. Jesus is the Light of the World. John said: "In the beginning was the Word, and the Word was with God, and the Word was God. The same was in the beginning with God. All things were made by him; and without him was not any thing made that was made. In him was life; and the life was the light of men. And the light shineth in darkness; and the darkness comprehended it not" (John 1:1–5).

Like John, my job is not to be the light. My job is to bear witness to the light of Jesus. My job is to tell somebody about the light. My job is to lift the light. My job is to tell somebody, "Don't look at me; look at the light." My job is to lift the light higher and higher and higher. Jesus said, "And I, if I be lifted up from the earth, will draw all men unto me" (John 12:32).

In case you're wondering what your job is, Jesus said: "Let your light so shine before men, that they may see your good works, and glorify your father which is in heaven" (Matt. 5:16).

When you live for Jesus, somebody sees your light and God gets the glory.

When you work for Him, somebody sees your light and God gets the glory.

When you serve Him, somebody sees your light and God gets the glory.

When you keep on climbing up the rough side of the mountain, somebody sees your light and God gets the glory.

When you praise Him, somebody sees your light and God gets the glory.

When you lift up holy hands, somebody sees your light and God gets the glory.

Jesus is the Light of the World.

In your dark days, He's the light.

In your midnight hours, He's the light.

On your gloomy days, He's the light.

When nights are long, He's the light.

When you cannot find a friend, He's the light.

When no one will stand by your side, He's the light.

When you're down and can't get up, He's the light.
When you cannot see your way, He's the light.

I heard the voice of Jesus say, I am this dark world's light.
Look unto me thy morn shall rise, and all thy days be bright.
I looked to Jesus and I found in Him my Star, my Sun;
And in that light of life I'll walk till traveling days are done.

Horatius Bonar

THE TABERNACLE
AND THE BREAD

God Still Feeds the Hungry
Exodus 25:29–30

And thou shalt make the dishes thereof, and spoons thereof, and covers thereof, and bowls thereof, to cover withal: of pure gold shalt thou make them. And thou shalt set upon the table shewbread before me alway. (Exod. 25:29–30)

And thou shalt take fine flour, and bake twelve cakes thereof: two tenth deals shall be in one cake. And thou shalt set them in two rows, six on a row, upon the pure table before the Lord. And thou shalt put pure frankincense upon each row, that it may be on the bread for a memorial, even an offering made by fire unto the Lord. Every sabbath he shall set it in order before the Lord continually. (Lev. 24:5–8)

Even the most casual observer of Scripture will note that Israel's building of the tabernacle of God was among the central themes in the Old Testament Book of Laws. Despite its prevalence in Scripture, however, for most of us, the tabernacle is dull subject matter. The tabernacle, with its construction, furnishings, symbols, shadows, word pictures, and typology, generally is not a topic from which devotional moments are drawn. To be sure, compared to seemingly more relevant events in our world that cause our collective pain and increase our fear, the tabernacle may not appear to be a worthy topic for a Sunday morning sermon. Nevertheless, I believe there is both meaning and strength in the tabernacle texts.

The meaning of the tabernacle, the center of Israel's worship, ought not be discounted or dismissed. The significance of the tabernacle, the place of Israel's spiritual gathering for nearly five hundred years, from the time of Moses until the time of David, ought not be ignored. So important is the tabernacle that the Bible devotes fifty chapters to its construction in both the Old and New Testaments.

Look with me, if you will, at the tabernacle. As you may have discovered, the tabernacle was constructed by Israel under the watchful eye of Moses, around 1450 BC. The tabernacle was not the work of fly-by-night contractors, but of skilled artisans and expert craftsmen who worked diligently according to the plans that were given to Moses by God at Mount Sinai.

The tabernacle was a portable structure that was transported for forty years in the wilderness and finally landed in Canaan, the land God promised the Israelites. You may remember that the tabernacle was only fifty-five feet in length and eighteen feet in breadth and height. This magnificent structure had walls that consisted of upright boards set in silver sockets with pillars and connecting bars overlaid with gold, giving the entire building the appearance of solid gold.

The walls were made up of curtains of fine, twisted linen with blue, purple, and scarlet embroidery on them. The entrance to the tabernacle was set at the eastern end and enclosed by draperies of costly material and exquisite workmanship. A brazen altar where sacrifices were made was located near the entrance to the court. Between the altar and the door of the tabernacle stood the brass laver, where the priests washed their hands and feet whenever they entered this sacred place or approached the altar to offer burnt offerings.

In addition to all of these things in this sacred place was a furnishing called the table of showbread. It is also called by other names in the Old Testament. In Numbers 4:7, it is called "the table of the Presence" (NIV), and in Leviticus 24:6 and 2 Chronicles 13:11, it is called the "pure table."

This table of showbread stood on the right side of the Holy of Holies in the tabernacle. It was a small table about three feet long, about a foot and a half wide, and about two feet, three inches high. It was made of acacia wood overlaid with gold. Twelve loaves of unleavened bread were placed in two rows on the showbread table, one for each of the twelve tribes of Israel. Also on the table were a pitcher of wine for drink offerings and pure frankincense. Every week on the Sabbath fresh loaves were placed on the table. Before worship could proceed, before sacrifices could be offered or hands lifted up in praise, one first had to stop by the table of showbread.

The Table of God's Presence

From the information I have given you so far, you may have been able to capture a vision of the table of showbread in your mind's eye. What is the meaning of this table with bread on it? The meaning lies in the fact that whenever the people of Israel gathered to worship, the worship experience was authentic only to the extent that Israel stood in God's presence. The table of showbread was a visible demonstration that they were in fact standing in the presence of God.

The tabernacle was first and foremost a place of worship. When engaged in worship, the worshiper was not concerned about how the worship surroundings looked, who was leading the worship, or how well printed the worship program was. The value of worship was always measured by whether or not the worshiper was in the presence of the one who is worthy of worship.

So it is for us. Worshiping is not simply coming into the presence of the priest. Worshiping is not simply coming in the presence of the Levite or the one who lifts up hymns and spiritual songs. True worship means standing in the presence of God.

When I come into a worship service, I need something to remind me that I am not simply standing in an auditorium. I need something that will let me know that I am standing in a holy place in the presence of God. When I come into a worship service, I need something to remind me that this is not just another gathering place that gets transformed for a few hours into a spiritualized arena. I need to know that there is something special about this place. I need to know that there is something God-ordained about this place and that angels hover here. I need to know that this is the place where from time to time there is a visitation of the supernatural, that every once in a while God himself comes calling. When I come into worship, I need something to remind me that this is not just fun and games, this is not an exercise in religious calisthenics. I am here because the living God has drawn me into His house where the cherubim and the seraphim cry out, "Holy, holy, holy." By this I know for myself that I am standing in the presence of God. The table of showbread reminded the people of Israel that for worship to truly be worship, God must be present.

The bread itself had meaning as well. The people of Israel were determined never to forget that during their wilderness experience God provided the bread they needed to eat when they needed to eat it. There were many other things that Israel did not have, but food was not one of them, because God provided bread every day. The showbread was called "bread of the face," because it had to be placed before the very face of God as a memorial to their hunger.

The showbread, then, was a symbol of Israel's hunger. Israel would never forget the days when they walked in the wilderness from sun up to sun down. They were a pilgrim people who could not stop long enough to plant and harvest crops. Thus, their supplies were meager, rations slim. The showbread would help them never to forget what it meant to be hungry.

I suspect you worship a little differently when you're hungry for God.

I suspect you approach Him a little differently when you're hungry.

I suspect you worship with greater intensity and listen to every word because you really want to know what God has to say that will affect your situation.

I also suspect that many of us today don't really know what it means to be hungry.

While we may not have experienced it ourselves, those of us who have been kissed with the indelible imprimatur of nature's sun should never forget the indignity of hunger that our ancestors suffered. Unlike us, during their forced exodus from the land of their birth to the land of their enslavement, our ancestors understood every day what it was to be hungry. Unlike them, we don't know what it means not to know where our next meal is coming from or if it is even coming at all.

God stepped in when Israel had nothing to eat. God—when food could not be found; God—when the wilderness had no meat and the vines yielded no grapes; God—when all Israel could remember was the food from Pharaoh's kitchen. God stepped in and fed Israel with manna from on high.

Crisis tends to make you grateful for the little things of life. Whenever you are hungry and someone feeds you, you tend not to forget it. That's not all. If you have ever been hungry, every time you sit down at the table to eat, you tend to remember how far the Lord has brought you. That's not all. Whenever you are hungry and realize there is more on your plate than you expected, you tend to remember that God is a good God. That's not all.

If you have ever been hungry, you tend to be thankful for whatever is put before you. When I was a child, I ate what Mama put on the table. We weren't allowed to say, "I don't like this" or "I don't like that." We were grateful for whatever we were given. There are times in your life when you have to be grateful for whatever is on your plate. If all you have on your plate is grits and grease, you need to be grateful. There comes a time when you have to thank God for the bread that is on your table!

In addition to being a symbol of Israel's hunger, the showbread was also a symbol of Israel's desire to be fed. When the people of Israel came into the tabernacle, they came to be fed. They were hungry and tired and needed to be fed. Yet their need for food was more than physical; it was also spiritual. The most seductive error in the interpretation of the bread is the temptation to see the bread as only a physical need and not as a spiritual need. I can have all the food I need in my refrigerator, but when I come into God's house, I have a hunger that food can't satisfy. I need spiritual manna from on high.

When my soul is hungry, I need to be fed. When my soul is hungry, I want to know "is there a word from the Lord?" When my soul is hungry, I want somebody to remind me that God still has fertile fields, green pastures, and still waters. When my soul is hungry, I want somebody to remind me that He who made both fish and fowl is still able to "prepare a table before me." I need to be fed.

When I come here I need to be fed. I don't come to be entertained. I come to be fed. I don't come here to hear the choir give a concert. I come to be fed. I don't come here to see the preacher put on a one-man show. I come to be fed. When I come here, I don't come to watch people jockey for seats and pretend to be important. I come to be fed.

When I consider the world in which I live, my spiritual health, not my physical health, is at risk. When I consider the fast-food diet this world serves, my mind, not my body, is at risk. I need to be fed from the rich resources of God's Word that let me know there is hope in history. I need to be fed from the rich resources of God's Word that let me know that God still has my world in His hands. I need to be fed from the rich resources of God's Word that let me know that even though war rises up against me, my heart has no need to fear. I need to be fed from the rich resources of God's Word that let me know that my "weeping may endure for a night but joy comes in the morning."

Israel came into the tabernacle rejoicing every time they saw the table of showbread, because it was both a symbol of their hunger and a visible reminder that in the presence of God they could be fed!

The Significance of Twelve

Here this word! There were twelve loaves of bread on the table of showbread, one for each of the tribes of Israel. That number has special significance in the Bible.

Jacob, or Israel, had twelve sons who were the heads of twelve tribes, and even Ishmael had twelve tribes descending from his twelve sons.

The priest in the tabernacle wore a breastplate with twelve stones. Joshua set up twelve stones in the River Jordan.

Solomon had twelve governors.

Elijah built an altar with twelve stones.

In the New Testament, Jesus was lost and found in the temple when He was twelve years old. Jesus had twelve disciples. After Jesus had finished feeding the five thousand, His disciples collected twelve baskets of leftovers.

In the book of Revelation, we discover that twelve kinds of fruit come from the tree of life and that the new Jerusalem has twelve gates inscribed with the names of the twelve tribes of Israel. Furthermore, the walls of the city have twelve foundations made of twelve different kinds of precious stones. John also said that he saw twenty-four elders around God's throne—two times twelve—who fell down and worshiped the living God. And in one place he saw 144,000 redeemed from the earth—twelve times twelve.

So then, the number twelve seems to represent completeness, and we have represented on the table of showbread all of the tribes of Israel. Everybody was represented; everybody was there.

Bread for Reuben—the son of a Syrian-Egyptian woman named Leah. He was Israel's firstborn son, born in both dignity and power.

Bread for Simeon and Levi—fierce and cruel brothers who took revenge against Shechem. They were neither righteous nor zealous for God's honor.

Bread for Judah—the fourth son of Jacob and Leah, a leader in family matters. Judah was the one who advised his brothers to throw Joseph into a pit, yet he was also the son who gained the first of Jacob's blessings.

Bread for Zebulun—the tenth of Jacob's sons, a dweller of the north country in Galilee, north of Carmel and the plain of Jezreel toward the Mediterranean coast.

Bread for Issachar—the son of Jacob who had an understanding of the times and who knew what Israel ought to do.

Bread for Dan—the son of Jacob and Bilhah, Rachel's servant. Dan's tribe was the tribe from which a man named Samson was born.

Bread for Gad—a full brother to Asher, both the sons of Zilpah, Leah's maid. Gad was awarded territory east of the Jordan on the condition that it would help other tribes in the conquest of Canaan.

Bread for Asher—the tribe who had it all and lost it. Asher, the largest of the twelve tribes, was given Palestine's richest territory but came to an inglorious end of inactivity and failure.

Bread for Naphtali—the son of Jacob and Bilhah, Rachel's servant, known as "a deer let loose."

Bread for Joseph—the favorite son of his father. Joseph was a "fruitful bow," industrous and reliable. He was an interpreter of dreams, energetic leader, and prime minister of Egypt.

Bread for Benjamin—the last of Jacob's sons, of whom it was said, "In the morning he shall devour the prey, and at night he shall divide the spoil" (Gen. 49:27).

No matter who they were, what their circumstances, how stained they were by the filth of the world, what their sin or their shame, when they got to the tabernacle, there was bread on the table.

You should know that there is more room at the table. No matter what your name, race, color, or ethnic origin may be, there's room for you at the table. You can come in from the exodus experience of your life—filthy or foul, vile or vilified, nasty or mean, a wretch undone—and still there's room for you at the table. Isaiah was right: "Though your sins be as scarlet, they shall be as white as snow; though they be red like crimson, they shall be as wool" (Isa. 1:18). And that's why there's showbread on the table.

The Source of Bread

There is one more facet of the showbread that we ought to consider. The showbread table was not designed to display the bread itself, but to point to the source of the bread. Israel needed more than bread, because if all they had was bread, that bread soon would have been consumed and the people would have withered and died. In a time of national crisis, Israel needed more than something fleeting; they needed an infinite, inexhaustible source of strength and power that would endure when everything else crumbled and fell.

John's gospel gives the account of a day when a crowd followed Jesus across the foothills of Palestine. Jesus had the people sit on a hillside so He could teach them. One of the disciples said to Him, "Jesus, the people are hungry, and we don't have anything to give them. The people are hungry, and we don't have any groceries. The people are hungry, and all we have is a boy's lunch of two little fish and five barley loaves."

When Jesus had fed the five thousand men and those with them, the disciples began to discuss the matter. They said, "Our fathers did eat manna in the desert; as it is written, He gave them bread from heaven to eat" (John 6:31).

And that's when Jesus told them that they shouldn't pattern themselves after their fathers. He reminded them that their fathers had eaten manna and were now dead. They needed more than manna. "I am the living bread which came down from heaven: if any man eat of this bread, he shall live for ever" (John 6:51). Jesus is the Bread of Life. Whatever you need, He is the bread. He will feed you when you're hungry.

David said, "I have never seen the righteous forsaken, nor his seed begging bread" (Ps. 37:25, my paraphrase). He will give you your daily bread. "My God shall supply all your need according to his riches in glory" (Phil. 4:19). He will prepare a table before you. "I am the living bread which came down from heaven: if any man eat of this bread, he shall live for ever." Go to the highways. Go to the hedges. There's more room at the table.

Go to that upper room in Jerusalem where Jesus, on the night before His crucifixion, took bread and broke it, saying, "This is my body which is given for you" (Luke 22:19). He is the bread. He will feed you till you want no more.

I'm on my way to the marriage supper of the Lamb. I'm on my way.

You can't feed me here. I'm on my way.

I'll leave the table over here because He has another table over there. I'm on my way.

Come over here where the table is spread and the feast of the Lord is going on!

The Tabernacle and the Mercy Seat

On Purposeful Worship
Exodus 25:17

And thou shalt make a mercy seat of pure gold: two cubits and a half shall be the length thereof, and a cubit and a half the breadth thereof. And thou shalt make two cherubims of gold, of beaten work shalt thou make them, in the two ends of the mercy seat. And make one cherub on the one end, and the other cherub on the other end: even of the mercy seat shall ye make the cherubims on the two ends thereof. And the cherubims shall stretch forth their wings on high, covering the mercy seat with their wings, and their faces shall look one to another; toward the mercy seat shall the faces of the cherubims be. And thou shalt put the mercy seat above upon the ark; and in the ark thou shalt put the testimony that I shall give thee. And there I will meet with thee, and I will commune with thee from above the mercy seat, from between the two cherubims which are upon the ark of the testimony, of all things which I will give thee in commandment unto the children of Israel. (Exod. 25:17–22)

The reasons we give for worshiping are broad and many. To be sure, there is nothing quite like this gathering, Sabbath upon Sabbath, that draws the faithful into a place called a sanctuary to engage in worship. There is something that compels us week after week to gravitate toward the singing and the praying, the preaching and the praising we call worship. It is not as if the experience is new. We have come here time and time again. It is not as if we really expect to see someone new. We have met on these same pews before. It is not as if we expect to hear something we have never heard. So repetitive is this preaching of ours that we call it an "old, old story."

And yet no matter what the reason we give for our gathering week after week, month after month, year after year, we come expecting something to happen. If not for ourselves, then perhaps for someone else sitting nearby, we expect something to happen. If we are not personally blessed, perhaps we will be in the vicinity of the blessing and be permitted to participate in a collateral shout. Surely there is nothing better than to be able to shout about a blessing that someone else has received.

Through worship we expect a divine-human connection. Through worship we expect that earth will get in touch with glory. Through worship we expect the finite to be able to catch a glimpse of the Infinite. Surely we expect an encounter, a hymn of hope, an anthem of praise, a soul set free, a healing touch, an anointing of oil, a sanctified shout, a wayfarer come home, or a *rhema* word from a prophet of God. We come here because we expect an epiphany, a revelation, or an incarnation. Whatever we may be looking for, we come expecting something to happen.

Terrence E. Fretheim, in the *Interpretation* commentary, suggests that to appropriately comprehend the book of Exodus, we must first understand the importance of worship: "The book of Exodus moves from slavery to worship, from Israel's bondage to Pharaoh to its bonding to Yahweh. More particularly, the book moves from the enforced construction of buildings for Pharaoh to the glad and obedient offering of the people for a building for the worship of God."[2]

In any analysis of the building of the tabernacle, therefore, it is important to understand that the tabernacle was constructed as a place for praise and worship.

The tabernacle's symbolism is in many ways hard to grasp, its typologies hard to comprehend. It is difficult to get an understanding of the hidden meanings of these symbols by simply reading the text. A casual reading of the text would not automatically bring one to the understanding that the bronze altar just beyond the entrance is there to demonstrate that Christ is our substitute and our sacrifice. The laver shows us that Christ cleanses us, regenerates us, and gives us new life. We might not glean that the showbread is designed to teach us to feed on Christ, who is the Bread of Life. Nor would we understand that the lampstand shows us that Christ is our light and our guide.

Who would know automatically that even the materials of the tabernacle speak of Jesus, the Christ? The wood speaks of humanity, the gold of His divinity. When you read about the colors that were used in the construction of the tabernacle, you would be hard pressed to know that white symbolizes purity; blue symbolizes promise and prophecy; purple bespeaks royalty, and red is for His blood.

In essence, this entire revelation of the tabernacle demonstrates that through Christ who "tabernacled" among us, we now have access to God, fellowship with the Father, the promise of eternal life, and citizenship in the kingdom of God. Apart from its symbolism, the tabernacle was constructed for the purpose of praise and worship to almighty God.

This idea of worship must be carefully considered. There is a great temptation to pause at the door and seek to worship there. Some will want to pause to worship near the bronze altar and marvel at its beauty. Others will perhaps want to come to church and pause near the showbread in order to be fed and, in being fed, worship. All of those places, however, represent the periphery of worship.

Pausing on the periphery of worship will always place you in the outer court rather than the inner court. If you simply remain by the door, the altar, the fire, the lampstand, or the bread, you will stand in awe of the instruments of worship. You will be caught up in the ambiance of worship; the majestic environment of worship will thrill you. Nevertheless, your worship will always be less than what God intended and less than what God requires.

When you choose to stay in the outer court of the tabernacle on the Sabbath Day, you run the risk of "worshiping worship." If I am worshiping worship, my name is on the roll and my body is on the premises. When I am worshiping worship, I attend church as a matter of habit and not because I am trying to live a holy life. When I am worshiping worship, I believe the presence of God will be conferred upon me by some process of transference or osmosis and not because I came for the purpose of entering into His presence and worshiping Him with my whole heart.

When I am worshiping worship, I remain quite alive for the singing of songs, the clapping of hands, and the dancing in the aisles. At the conclusion of those strenuous spiritual calisthenics, however, I soon fall fast asleep during the waste of time called "offering" and the intermission called "sermon." When I am worshiping worship, I am more concerned about who is singing and who is attending and who is seated on my pew than I am about making a connection with the God of my salvation, whose assured presence brought me here in the first place.

The Outer Court

To make this concept come alive, let's look more closely at the tabernacle's outer court. The tabernacle was divided into two chambers or courts. The Holy Place, or outer court, was the place of frequent visitation. The outer court contained among other things the lampstand, the table of showbread, the bronze altar, and the incense altar. Beyond the altar of incense and the veil was the Holy of Holies, which contained the ark of the covenant, a gold-covered chest designed to house the two stone tablets of the law God had given Moses on Sinai, the hidden manna God had provided the children of Israel on their march from slavery to freedom, and Aaron's rod of budding almonds. On top of the ark of the covenant was a solid gold cover called the mercy seat, which held two golden images of cherubim.

Once a year the high priest made his way into the Holy of Holies and sprinkled blood of atonement on the mercy seat to take away the sins of the people and of his own house. The cherubim, facing each other and looking toward the cover, had their wings spread upward, overshadowing the cover.

When the priest stood in the presence of the ark, he was standing in a holy place. Similarly, when I come to worship, I want to know that I am standing in a holy place, because worship is not worship unless I am standing in a holy place.

When I come to worship, I want to know that I am in a place God frequents.

When I come to church, I want to know that I am not just in another building, auditorium, or amphitheater.

I want to know that in whatever building I am standing, a transformation has taken place.

If I worship in a storefront, I want to know that this is a storefront where the Living God tends to traffic.

I want to know that I am standing in a place where things happen that do not happen anywhere else.

I want to know that I am in a place where angels are hovering.

I want to be in a place where burdens get lifted, wounds get healed, depression is dismissed, poverty is rebuked, lives get changed, joy is restored, and an anointing flows from the crown of my head to the soles of my feet.

Yes, I want to know that I am standing in a holy place.

For the children of Israel, the mercy seat was the place where God met with the people through the high priest. It was at the mercy seat that God made himself manifest. You didn't have to search for God; if you wanted to find Him, you could find Him at the mercy seat.

When I was a child, people didn't talk about going to church; they talked about going to the "meetin'." In fact, when you got dressed on Sunday morning, you put on your "Sunday-go-to-meetin'" clothes. They were going to a place where they could meet, or have a meeting with, God. I don't want to just go to church; I want to go to a meeting. I want to meet the God of my salvation. I want to meet the one who blew breath into my body. I want to meet the one who put activity in my limbs. I want to meet the one who put me to sleep last night and then woke me up this morning in time and not in eternity. I want to meet the one who feeds me, cleanses me, clothes me, watches over me, provides for me, and loves me when I don't know how to love myself.

The only way I know I've been to worship is that at some time during the process I have met God for myself. For that reason, I must engage in purposeful worship, which requires that I know I'm in a holy place where I can meet God for myself.

I Know It Was the Blood

Let's dig a little deeper. The ark of the covenant had a golden cover called the mercy seat. Cherubim were situated at both ends of the ark on the mercy seat. The Hebrew says their four wings were "stretched out" to provide a covering or protective shield. From where they were situated with their wings stretched out, the cherubim looked down upon the cover where the atoning blood had been sprinkled.

Surely, whenever the high priest made his way into the Holy of Holies to sprinkle the atoning blood, Israel remembered that night when God sent word for them to put blood on the doorposts of their homes during what became the Passover. Like Israel, if you have blood on your doorposts—that is, if your sins have been atoned for by the blood of Jesus—when the death angel passes over, you will be covered by the blood. The blood was a sign of a continuing relationship of redemption between God and His people.

Just as the lamb's blood covered Israel, Jesus' blood covers you. In today's fragile world, we need to be reminded that we must be covered by the blood. In fact, whether you know it or not, the only reason you're alive with blood running warmly through your veins is because you've been covered by Jesus' blood. Every time I see the news photos of those planes crashing into the twin towers in New York, I can't help but think that there but for the grace of God go I. Thankfully, I've been covered by Jesus' blood. Not only the few who were saved, but I believe that even those who may have lost their lives by an act of heartless insanity, in a moment of time— they too were covered by the blood.

Apart from the blood of Jesus, I wouldn't have any right to make my way into the Holy of Holies. I would be kept on the outside because of my sin stains. But Jesus has made a way for me to enter into God's presence with confidence. No, I'm not perfect, but I am covered by the blood. And you're not perfect either. But, yes, you are covered by the blood.

That's why when I come to worship my goal is to get to the mercy seat.

When I recognize where I've been, I need to get to the mercy seat.

When I recognize my sins and shortcomings, I need to get to the mercy seat.

When I recognize my faults and failures, I need to get to the mercy seat.

The mercy seat is the cover that intercedes between me and the punishment I deserve.

I need mercy. We all need mercy.

"For all have sinned, and come short of the glory of God" (Rom. 3:23). I need mercy.

I was born in iniquity; in sin did my mother conceive me. I need mercy.

My sin is red like crimson; my sin is just like scarlet. I need mercy.

When I would do good, evil is always before me. I need mercy.

"O wretched man that I am! who shall deliver me from the body of this death?" (Rom. 7:24). I need mercy.

Mercy came and made the difference one Friday at the cross! "Behold, the veil of the temple was rent in twain from the top to the bottom; and the earth did quake, and the rocks rent." (Matt. 27:51). Because of Jesus, I can make my way into the Holy of Holies. Because of Jesus, I don't have to stand on the outside looking in. Because of Jesus, I don't have to stay in the outer court; I can come on in to the inner court. "Let us therefore come boldly unto the throne of grace, that we may obtain mercy, and find grace to help in time of need" (Heb. 4:16).

I looked at the cherubim again, and this is what I learned. In the process of spreading their wings and covering the mercy seat, they kept their eyes on the blood. When the priest came in, they did not put their eyes on the priest, they kept their eyes on the blood. And so the only way to engage in purposeful worship is to keep your eyes on the blood.

> *The blood that Jesus shed for me,*
> *Way back on Calvary,*
> *The blood that gives me strength*
> *From day to day,*
> *It will never lose its power.*

Andraé Crouch

In Search of Shekinah Glory

When God Comes to Worship

Exodus 40:34

Then a cloud covered the tent of the congregation, and the glory of the Lord filled the tabernacle. And Moses was not able to enter into the tent of the congregation, because the cloud abode thereon, and the glory of the Lord filled the tabernacle. And when the cloud was taken up from over the tabernacle, the children of Israel went onward in all their journeys: But if the cloud were not taken up, then they journeyed not till the day that it was taken up. For the cloud of the Lord was upon the tabernacle by day, and fire was on it by night, in the sight of all the house of Israel, throughout all their journeys. (Exod. 40:34–38)

And on the day that the tabernacle was reared up the cloud covered the tabernacle, namely, the tent of the testimony: and at even there was upon the tabernacle as it were the appearance of fire, until the morning. (Num. 9:15)

At the point of our text, the tabernacle God had Israel build had been completed. Grand and glorious was this holy place, this tent of meeting Israel would enter for worship and praise. The work of Israel's craftsmen was beautifully detailed. Every specification, no matter how slight, had been met. The door, the lampstand, the brazen altar, the altar of incense, the table of showbread, the laver, the ark of the covenant with the mercy seat—all the furniture that God had specified and designed—was now in place. There was no place like this place, and Israel had built it by sacrificing all they possessed. The people of God had brought gold, silver, brass, dyed ram skins, costly fabric, shittim wood, oil, spices, and anointing oil, not to mention precious stones for the ephod and breastpiece—the best they had—for building God's tabernacle. Moses' task was finished. God is not a God of the incomplete. The plan was fulfilled; the vision had become reality. In every detail, the tabernacle that God had Israel build was now complete.

When the Work Is Complete

Anyone who has ever led a project from start to finish knows that the time of completion was a moment of incomparable joy for a stammering preacher named Moses. Consider Moses' predicament. Before Moses was born, Pharaoh had declared that all male Hebrew babies should die. Before Moses could be weaned from his mother's breast, he was set afloat in the Nile River, left to fend for himself wrapped in a blanket in a basket. God arranged for him to be rescued by the daughter of the man who wanted to kill him and made a way for him to be cared for by Jochebed, his birth mother, reared and groomed in Pharaoh's palace, and then, of all things, to stand in line as Pharaoh's son to become a pharaoh.

While in Pharaoh's service, Moses could not forget who he was. In some midnight moment, Jochebed had taught him never to forget that no matter how far he rose in Pharaoh's house, he was still a slave. When he saw an Egyptian taskmaster abusing a Hebrew slave, Moses killed him and hid the body in the sand. God put Moses on parole and left him on the back side of a desert to tend sheep for his father-in-law, Jethro.

While tending sheep on Sinai, God arranged for Moses to encounter a bush that was on fire but did not burn. God then sent this fugitive from justice back to Egypt to tell Pharaoh, "Let my people go." God sent Moses with nothing but a stick in his hand and told him to lead Israel from slavery to freedom. Moses had no identifiable leadership skills, had never taken a single course in management, and had no strategic plan for his assignment. He was understaffed and undercapitalized and had learned all that he knew as a result of on-the-job training. God set him up then sent him out with two million people behind him, a number that included 603,550 fighting men carrying everything they owned in the world. His assignment was to lead two million people approximately three hundred miles through a wilderness, without a road map or directions from the Internet, to a place called the Promised Land, a place none of the travelers had ever been to before.

The people of Israel did not want to enter the Promised Land because they were afraid of what lay ahead. Because of their disobedience and lack of trust, God let them wander in the desert instead. They murmured, complained, and wanted to go back to Egypt where the food tasted better. When Moses woke up to pray, his so-called followers rose up to play. They did not know why they had to follow this wandering nomad of a preacher, the "Reverend Doctor Bishop Pastor Moses."

In the midst of it all, Moses told the people that God had given him a vision for building a portable place of worship. He said that God had told him, "Speak unto the children of Israel, that they bring me an offering. . . . And let them make me a sanctuary; that I may dwell among them" (Exod. 25:2, 8).

When you understand all that Moses and the Israelites had to go through to get to this place, perhaps you will then grasp the significance of the moment that found them putting the finishing touches on their work. The tabernacle that God had instructed them to build was now nearly complete. I say "nearly," because while it was complete in its physical dimensions, it was not yet complete in its spiritual dimensions. The instruction was to build the tabernacle so that God could dwell there.

A church is not a church until God decides that it will become a place of divine visitation. The building may be one of architectural splendor and exquisite design, but it is not a church until God issues a "certificate of divine occupancy" and takes up residence there.

Then

Here's what happened after the tabernacle was complete. Exodus 40:34 says, "Then a cloud covered the tent of the congregation, and the glory of the LORD filled the tabernacle."

Then—after everything else was completed.

Then—when the assigned task had reached its fulfillment.

Then—when God's instructions had been meticulously followed.

Then the glory of the Lord filled the tabernacle.

"The glory of the LORD" is the important phrase in this text. It is not just any glory; it is *the* glory, the Shekinah glory, as distinguished from any other kind of glory.[3] The word *Shekinah* comes from a biblical concept that describes the presence of Yahweh in a certain location. *Shekinah* was derived from the word *shakan* and is used to describe the abiding, dwelling, or habitation of the physical manifestations of God in the time-space continuum. The word *mishkan* is a derivation of *shakan* and is the Hebrew word for tabernacle. *Mishkan,* therefore, means dwelling place or the "dwelling place of him who dwells." In other words, the local address of the God of the cosmos is Shekinah.

Let's look at it another way. The Hebrew verb *shakan* simply means to take up residence in a neighborhood for a long period of time. When God is *shakan,* it means that He is dwelling long-term in the midst of a neighborhood or group of people.

Let's examine the concept further. Shekinah is defined as "the Divine Presence, . . . the numinous immanence of God in the world, . . . a revelation of the holy in the midst of the profane."[4] The Shekinah, which in its physical dimension consisted of cloud and fire, was the evidence that God, whom Israel had known as omnipresent but had not seen, was in fact real. The Shekinah glory was, then, a physical manifestation of God's actual presence among His people. The Shekinah was not God; it was the instrument to enable us to know and experience God.

Therefore, when Moses asked to see the glory of God, he was shown the Shekinah. When prophets saw God in human form in their visions, they did not see God himself. Rather, they saw the Shekinah. When the children of Israel set out from Succoth in their escape from Egypt, a cloudy pillar led them by day and a fiery pillar led them by night. That was the Shekinah.

The book of Exodus says that when the children of Israel crossed the Red Sea, God looked down from a pillar of fire and cloud at the Egyptian army and threw it into confusion. He made the wheels of their chariots come off so that they had difficulty driving. That was the Shekinah glory. During the forty years the children of Israel were in the wilderness, the Shekinah glory went before them and rested above them.

Now that the tabernacle was finished, now that the assigned task had been fulfilled, now that God's instructions had been meticulously followed, God came calling. And the Bible says that the glory of the Lord—the Shekinah glory—filled the tabernacle.

On Clouds and Fire

Some people may think it peculiar that the church is following a cloud. They think the church should be dealing with substantive, critical issues rather than following a cloud. They accuse the church of being irrelevant and having their heads in the clouds. They accuse the church of trying to go to a heaven out there when folks in the pews are living in hell down here. Following a cloud in this day and age appears impractical, unrealistic, and irrelevant. With issues such as poverty and pain confronting us within a pathless and dangerous wilderness, it seems insane that the church should follow a cloud. When wars and rumors of wars are upon us, when we live every day under the threat of biological warfare or nuclear destruction, why is the church following a cloud?

The truth of the matter is that the church does not follow a cloud; the church follows the one who caused the cloud to form. The church is not fixated on fire; the church is caught up in the one who put the heat in the fire. The cloud and the fire confirm that we are not alone. The cloud reveals that in the daytime you can look up and find assurance in God's presence. The fire reveals that in the nighttime when it gets dark and cold and you cannot see your way, God's presence will be with you. The invisible manifestation of God, the Shekinah glory is always with us.

Yes, I'm in search of Shekinah glory today. I have seen a lot of churches, but I'm searching for a church that is marked by the Shekinah glory. I have been in churches that are architecturally breathtaking. I have been to St. Paul's in London, St. Peter's in Rome, and the Cathedral of Notre Dame in Paris. I have even been to Metropolitan in Washington. But when I go to church, I'm looking for the Shekinah glory. I have been in churches where the praise music was splendid, the preaching of the Word was incomparable, and the priests were gowned in opulent ecclesiastical finery. But what I'm looking for is not just a church that is exquisite on the outside; I'm looking for a church that has something uncommon at work on the inside. I'm not looking for an ecclesiastical, spiritualized sideshow. I'm looking for something real. I'm looking for something tangible. I'm looking for something I can take hold of and that will ultimately take hold of me. I'm looking for a manifestation of the eternal and everlasting God. Yes, I'm in search of the Shekinah glory.

Shekinah Glory

The traditional interpretation of Shekinah glory suggests that it is a manifestation to be experienced in the context of worship. It is interpreted as a powerful spiritual presence experienced in Sabbath day exercises. We go to church, and the Shekinah glory shows up. But the Bible says that the Shekinah glory showed up while Israel was on the way to the Red Sea and stayed with Israel during their wilderness journey. While the Shekinah glory was manifested when Israel completed the tabernacle, it also showed up during their journey through the wilderness. The exodus narrative shows us then that the God who shows up in your worship will first show up in your wilderness.

He will show up when your life is in danger.

He will show up in your lonely, desert place.

He will show up when you are in deep water and about to go down for the third time.

The Shekinah glory is "the shade upon your right hand" that allows you to know that "the sun will not smite you by day nor the moon by night." Just when you need God—anytime you need Him—He is always there. In fact, the reason you have made it through your experience of slavery, across your Red Sea, through your wanderings and your own wilderness is because the Shekinah glory is always there right on time.

To be successful in this search for Shekinah glory, God's people must be willing to follow wherever He leads. Israel's trouble from beginning to end was that Israel wanted to go where Israel wanted to go. Once Israel had escaped Egypt and made it through the Red Sea on dry ground, they would no longer follow the vision God had for them. That's why we refer to their experience as "wilderness wandering."

Whenever your vision for yourself is inconsistent with God's vision for you, the result is wandering.

Whenever you insist on living your life according to your plans rather than surrendering your life to God's plan, the result is wandering.

High school geometry teaches you that the shortest distance between two points is a straight line. But if God is not in charge of that line, the result is wandering.

Israel's Wandering and Ours

One lesson to be learned from Exodus and Numbers is that God does not wander. The children of Israel wandered, but God does not wander. A careful reading of the book of Numbers shows that the children of Israel started their wandering at Kadesh. In fact, they wandered through the wilderness for thirty-eight years. Yet when their wandering years were over and they came back to Kadesh, they found that the cloud was still there waiting to lead them into the land God had promised.

Understand that God has a place and a purpose toward which He intends to direct His people. God is not lost. God knows where He is going. You can wander all you want, but the Shekinah glory you needed when you started will be there to meet you when you get back. To get out of your wilderness and find yourself in right relationship with Him, to search out and find the Shekinah glory, you must let Him lead.

Exodus 40:30–33 teaches us another lesson about the Shekinah glory. Before the Shekinah glory came to the tabernacle, a cleansing process took place. The tabernacle included an item of furniture called the laver. The laver was there for worshipers who came from their wilderness to wash before they stood in God's presence. It is clear from our text that before the Shekinah glory came, a cleansing process had to take place.

Likewise, before we search for the Shekinah glory, we should look within ourselves to be sure that some cleansing has taken place.

When I consider the world in which I live and the wilderness through which I have come, I need to be cleansed.

When I consider the mud and the filth of life through which I have come, I need to be cleansed.

When I consider where I've been and what I've done, the sin, the stain, the dirt on my shoes, and the soil on my hands, I need to be cleansed.

There is no one who doesn't need this cleansing. Even the apostle Paul had to come clean. He confessed, "For the good that I would I do not: but the evil which I would not, that I do. . . . O wretched man that I am!" (Rom. 7:19, 24). For the Shekinah glory to come, you need to come clean. Even King David had to come clean. He prayed, "Purge me with hyssop, and I shall be clean: wash me, and I shall be whiter than snow. Create in me a clean heart, O God; and renew a right spirit within me. Cast me not away from thy presence; and take not thy holy spirit from me. Restore unto me the joy of thy salvation; and uphold me with thy free spirit" (Ps. 51:7, 10–12).

A third lesson we can learn about the Shekinah glory is that when the glory comes, titles don't count. When the children of Israel became obedient and let God lead, when they decided that God was not lost, when they discovered that God would show up in their wilderness as well as in their worship, and when they had gone through their cleansing process, the Shekinah glory descended upon the tabernacle. The text says: "Then a cloud covered the tent of the congregation, and the glory of the LORD filled the tabernacle. And Moses was not able to enter into the tent of the congregation, because the cloud abode thereon, and the glory of the LORD filled the tabernacle" (Exod. 40:34–35).

When the Shekinah glory came down, the temple-dwellers and tabernacle-goers attempted to enter, but God's presence was so strong that no seats were available; the Shekinah glory had filled the tabernacle. It didn't make any difference who you were. Even Moses couldn't get in.

When God shows up in the tabernacle, titles don't count.

When the Shekinah glory shows up, all the church bigwigs have to get in line with everybody else.

When the Shekinah glory shows up, all the preachers parading in the pulpit join the ranks of the unemployed.

The Shekinah glory serves as a reminder that nobody but God is in charge of the worship.

When the Shekinah glory comes, the bulletin can be thrown away and the preacher can throw his sermon away, because God can do the preaching for himself.

When the Shekinah glory comes, you won't need your choir robe anymore.

In fact, when the Shekinah glory comes, you won't need the choir anymore, because angels will be everywhere singing, "Holy, holy, holy."

When God's glory comes, it fills the house. There is glory in the pulpit and the pew.

Glory will get in the ushers.

Glory will get in the choir.

Glory will be on the front row.

Glory will be on the back row.

Glory will get in the balcony.

Glory will be everywhere.

All God requires is that you are willing to build the tabernacle. God remains available to lead you through your wilderness until you arrive at a promised land designed for you according to His purpose and His plan. If you are obedient and just try to get to the tabernacle and take yourself through the cleansing process, you will become the tabernacle. Paul raised the question, "Know ye not that ye are the temple of God, and that the Spirit of God dwelleth in you?" (1 Cor. 3:16).

The tabernacle of God is not made of stone; it's in you. God doesn't need a building; He already has all the buildings He needs. Psalm 24:1 says, "The earth is the LORD's, and the fulness thereof; the world, and they that dwell therein." God wants you. Every specification for the tabernacle is a design He has for you.

God has a vision for your life. He wants the door to your heart. He wants a sacrificial spirit. He wants to be the light and the lamp-stand of your soul. He wants to be bread when you're hungry, fire when you're cold, a laver when you're dirty, and mercy in the time of your deepest need. He wants to cover you with His blood and then send cherubim to watch over you all night long. The tabernacle He is building is the tabernacle in you.

God doesn't just want you to build a church; God wants to be a tabernacle in you.

A complete understanding of the clouds and fire isn't necessary. All you need to know is that God wants to be a cloud hovering over you.

I want a cloud over me.

When I walk the streets of this city, I want a cloud over me.

When I stand before men and nations, I want a cloud over me.

With sickness everywhere I look, I want a cloud over me.

With pain surrounding me everywhere I go, I need a cloud over me.

When I get lonely, when I'm in despair, I want a cloud over me.

When enemies and foes come upon me, I want a cloud over me.

I don't just want a cloud; I want fire too!

Fire over me to purify me.

Fire over me to separate me.

Fire over me to energize me.

Fire over me to be my light in dark places.

Fire over me to warm me up when nights are cold.

Fire over me to set my soul ablaze.

Fire over me—a prayer wheel turning, a fire burning.

Fire over me so the Holy Ghost can take control.

Fire over me so the Shekinah glory can preach in my place.

Fire over me so when I come to this pulpit you don't come to hear me preach, but you come to watch me burn up.

Fire over me!

DO YOU SEE WHAT I SEE?

Be careful with the Moses paradigm. It is tempting to view one-self as a daring Moses, full beard, robes flapping in the wind, walking staff at the ready, with thousands following in one's wake. It is heady stuff to think that God has specially chosen you to speak for Him, or to be the one chosen to communicate with the great I Am, or to be the one able to see the Glory pass while you are hidden behind a rock, or to lead God's people from one place to the next. The temptation is that those who must follow us may also be tempted to see us as larger than life—a caricature of a self we are straining to become but have not reached. To be used by God as Moses was used is at once an awesome charge and an awful burden.

There is really only one sense in which we stand in the Moses tradition. We are each assigned to desert duty. The craft of preaching and ministry are worked out in the desert—some lonely assignment that does not make sense to those whom we lead and often does not make sense to us. It is in this desert, however, that we come face-to-face with certain realities.

First, that we are inadequate to the task.

Second, that we cannot achieve either the goal or the vision without divine intervention.

Third, that our symbol of authority is never a scepter; it is always a stick.

We preach because that is as God intended. When Moses complained that his oratorical skills were not sufficient, God explained that his greatest achievements would not come as a consequence of his strategic plan or his as-yet-undeveloped leadership skills. Moses is chosen and commissioned to lead Gods people because God would be in his mouth:

> Now therefore go, and I will be with thy mouth,
> and teach thee what thou shalt say. (Exod. 4:12)

One day the desert; next day the pulpit. One day shepherding in the wilderness; next day preaching in Pharaoh's house. God chooses, as incredible as it may seem, to lead his people through words that come out of our mouths.

It is in the desert that the chosen of God learn the necessary lessons about appropriate uses of power and how to exercise authority. My grandfather, the Reverend William Hicks, spoke of leadership in this way: "You can draw them but you can never drive them." We lead and draw by example, by taking the first step into the water, by being the testament of the word you preach. Remember that in the desert there is no place for the imperial pastorate. Authority is the by-product of service and trust. As we serve our people, they will come to trust us and, in trusting, give us the sufficient authority we will need to guide them to the Land of Promise.

Is all this really true? Does any of this really work?

In the first year of my pastorate in a small church in upstate New York, I was called to the bedside of a beloved deacon who was near the point of death. Doctors said his coma was irreversible and it was only a matter of time. I stood at Deacon Burrell's bedside and gently called his name. Miraculously, he turned, opened his eyes, and looked straight at me. He spoke with a clear voice: "Reverend. You can't make me doubt Him!" And he closed his eyes in sleep.

God is faithful to his Word. God is faithful to his promise. You must trust that faithfulness even when it seems that none of this is true. He who calls you to the desert is faithful to bring you through the desert. You can't make me doubt Him!

PREACHING
the VISION

PART IV

THE TABERNACLE RESPONSE

Sermons that are preached only as a matter of course are both life-less and meaningless. Sermons preached without any effect on either ear or heart are like trees falling in the woods when no one is around, leaving one wondering if any sound was ever made or heard. On the contrary, sermons ought to gain a response from the hearers—not only verbal response, but a living response manifested in a change in belief and behavior.

In the African American tradition, the sermonic hour is filled with what is called "call and response." The message of the priest-watchperson is affirmed through the sermon by direct and audible responses from the congregation. This response may seem to some as a meaningless, even distracting, idiosyncrasy of the church. Yet the practice of call and response has biblical imperative and today retains its significance. Every preacher listens for the "amen," the word that declares the preacher is "on point." Every preacher wants to know that the church is in agreement with the thesis of the ser-mon and is benefiting spiritually.

Unfortunately, in the contemporary church, the vocal "amen" is in danger of being replaced with applause. Nevertheless, the preacher who stands to preach in silence is sad indeed, because it is through call and response that the watchperson knows that his or her word is received and understood.

What then was the Metropolitan congregation's response to the sermons preached about the tabernacle? Did the sermons achieve the desired effect of casting the vision so that the congregation could accept it and buy into it? Did a consensus emerge among the congregation that the word being preached was appropriate and relevant to the church's needs? Or was there a still silence that came over the congregation, a kind of patient endurance with the hope that next Sunday the preacher would abandon this notion and get on with the "real gospel"? Did the sermons anger the congregation such that they could not hear what was being said because of all the negative emotions they felt? Did these sermons elicit a powerful response among the people or change opinions? Was there a shift in the perception of relevancy or importance of the vision, or was there a silent thud as the word of the preacher fell weakly and harmlessly to the sanctuary floor? Finally, did the sermons provide as intended a theological and biblical foundation upon which vision casting would be built in the weeks and months to come?

The answer to all of these questions is "yes." That is to say, the sermons received mixed reviews. For some, the struggle was not with God or God's Word but with God's spokesman, whose communication strategies were at times something less than effective. For others, the struggle was among themselves, in an internal dialogue that perhaps went "underground" and never found full expression in the church as a whole. Yet there was and remains a "remnant"—those who hear and receive the vision and give of themselves and their resources to bring it to life. Through this struggle it is apparent that God is raising up a new generation in the church that is determined to be faithful to the vision that He has so clearly given.

On Sunday, November 17, 2002, the Metropolitan congregation was challenged to bring pledge commitments for the erection of a new tabernacle for Christ. Commitments to this campaign have been more than substantial.

TOO MUCH STUFF

Just Look at God!

Exodus 36:4–7

And all the wise men, that wrought all the work of the sanctuary, came every man from his work which they made; and they spake unto Moses, saying, The people bring much more than enough for the service of the work, which the Lord commanded to make. And Moses gave commandment, and they caused it to be proclaimed throughout the camp, saying, Let neither man nor woman make any more work for the offering of the sanctuary. So the people were restrained from bringing. For the stuff they had was sufficient for all the work to make it, and too much. (Exod. 36:4–7)

If anyone had told the people of Israel that they could build a tabernacle in a dry and barren wilderness, they wouldn't have believed it. If anyone had ever told them that their worship would be held in anything other than a portable tent with a temporary altar, the cries of utter disbelief would have been deafening. If anyone had ever told them that God had a vision that would change their history and redirect their destiny in such a tremendous way, they would have been laughed to scorn.

Yet that was the very word they got. You know these people— the descendants of Abraham, Isaac, and Jacob. Not only do you know them, but you know the reason they were where they were. Famine had struck Egypt and the neighboring lands, but Egypt had stockpiled grain, so Jacob sent his sons to Egypt to buy some. Joseph (the same Joseph in the Technicolored coat who had been sold into slavery by his brothers), by a set of divinely ordained circumstances, wound up as secretary of agriculture in Egypt just in time to provide food for his brothers. But then a pharaoh rose up in Egypt who had not heard of Joseph, and four hundred years of bitter bondage and excruciating slavery of the Israelites ensued.

God heard the cries of His enslaved people and sent a deliverer in the form of a baby born in the ghetto of Goshen—Moses. After his mother placed him in a basket and set him afloat in the Nile River in an effort to keep him from being killed according to Pharaoh's orders to kill all male Hebrew babies, he was rescued by Pharaoh's daughter. He grew up in Pharaoh's palace, was trained by Pharaoh's tutors, and dined at Pharaoh's table. Then one day, after Moses had been exiled in the desert for murdering an Egyptian who had mistreated a fellow Hebrew, God met with him on a mountain called Sinai. There He gave Moses one sermon to preach: "Moses, tell Pharaoh, 'Let my people go!'"

Not long after that, Moses was leading a band of refugees carrying all of their worldly goods in their wagons or on their backs to a land that God would show them. Soon this group of travelers found themselves standing at the edge of the Red Sea with death by water before them and death by Pharaoh's soldiers behind them. But then God stepped in on time and pushed back the water so that it stood at attention while the children of Israel walked across on dry ground. From that moment on, the people of Israel were on their way to the Promised Land, secured for them by God.

So there they were—wanderers, nomads, exiles smelling of sheep and goats. They did not know where they were going. They had no clue what they were doing. They had no strategic plan. They had no economic resources. Without a doubt, they were the poorest of the poor. Their days were dry and hot; their nights were long and cold. Their tongues were parched, and their feet were sore. Their diet consisted of quail and heaven-sent bread called manna. Because of their disobedience they were engaged in the largest traveling travesty known to humankind. They were literally going around and around in circles, never finding what they were looking for, always uncertain of how to get to their destination, and always winding up back where they first started.

It was under these circumstances that God gave Moses an incredible task, an enormous responsibility, a grand vision: He was to tell the people of Israel that God wanted them to build a sanctuary. "And the LORD spake unto Moses, saying, Speak unto the children of Israel, that they bring me an offering: of every man that giveth it willingly with his heart ye shall take my offering. . . . And let them make me a sanctuary; that I may dwell among them" (Exod. 25:1–2, 8).

Let's see if we understand this. In the middle of a desert, under the worst conditions possible, God said, "Build me a sanctuary." With people who were ill-prepared, with a community that was on shaky spiritual ground, and with leadership that was split from top to bottom, God said, "Build me a sanctuary."

Given these circumstances, there were several reasons why God's directive, "Build me a sanctuary," didn't seem feasible. First, it wouldn't work because of the demographic realities Moses faced. He was dealing with inexperienced people. The longer he stayed in the wilderness, the more he realized that the people he started out with were dying and that he had a whole new breed of people with whom he had no relationship. He was dealing with people who were themselves displaced, always on the move and living in tents. They had no history of stable living conditions. How could they have been expected to build a house for God when they had little or no experience of living in their own houses? And if that were not enough, they were ex-slaves. They barely had tasted the sweet waters of liberty and freedom for themselves. Furthermore, they had no experience whatsoever in building sanctuaries. And you mean to tell me that God said, "Let them make me a sanctuary"? Anyway you look at it, it wouldn't work.

The second reason God's directive wouldn't work was because Israel had a leadership problem. They had a leader they had not chosen. Moreover, they had a leader nobody else would have chosen. He was not a good communicator; he stuttered when he talked. He was not a good role model or moral example; he had killed an Egyptian and then tried to hide his sin in the sand. No matter how you try to fix it up or clean it up, Moses was a murderer in exile. As far as the children of Israel were concerned, whatever plan Moses had was suspect. His credibility was further compromised when the people realized that he had no experience in sanctuary building. He was in well over his head.

This just wouldn't work. Not only were the demographics disastrous, not only did the Israelites have a leader they did not choose, but as far as they could tell, Moses wanted them to build this sanctuary in the worst possible location. They could have understood if He had wanted to build it back in Goshen where they had already been for four hundred years. They had been the lead church in downtown Goshen. They had history in that place. Their enslaved ancestors had built it, and the whole fabric of the community had been built around it. If they had just stayed where they were, they would have been all right. But this upstart Moses wanted to move out beyond the borders of tradition from the known to the unknown, beyond the comfort zone of traditional religion to a place they had never seen and did not know, among people they had never met. They had been in the city, but Moses wanted to move to the suburbs. As far as they could tell, it was dry and arid wasteland. They could not understand why God needed to have a tabernacle there.

Look again at the difficulties the Israelites were facing when God, in the middle of the desert, said, "Let them make me a sanctuary." Demographics were disastrous, the leader was unfit, and the chosen location seemed the worst possible. If all of that were not enough, Moses was faced with an impossible economic climate. The people of Israel were broke. The stock market had been playing teeter-totter with their money, and nobody knew what the economic future would hold. Interest rates were low and jobs were scarce; people were living on limited resources and fixed incomes.

The people wondered how Rev. Moses could speak of building sanctuaries in such grave economic times. Had he counted the cost and considered the economic consequences of this venture? "Rev. Moses, this thing is apt to cost more money than we can count. We want to know if you had a vision or nightmare. Did God really say do this, or is that just you talking? We want to be sure it was really God who said, 'Let them make me a sanctuary.'"

Willing Hearts

At the point of our text, the building of the sanctuary is about to commence. To gain an understanding of what is going to happen in chapter 36, you must take a moment to read chapter 35. There you will discover that the people brought the materials necessary for the construction of the sanctuary: gold, silver, brass, fine linen, goats' hair, ram skins dyed red, badger skins, shittim wood, oil for the light, spices for anointing oil, onyx stones, stones for the ephod and the breastplate, and more. Despite seemingly insurmountable challenges, the people of Israel gathered what they needed to build a sanctuary.

I am sure you are curious about the strategy the Israelites used to overcome challenges that would seem to preclude them from accomplishing this awesome task. You will discover in Exodus 35:5 that they brought an offering to the Lord with a "willing heart." Moses didn't have to beg. He didn't have to fry any chicken. He didn't have to sell any tickets. He didn't have to ask them over and over again. They knew what God was requiring of them, and they brought their offerings with willing hearts.

God can't use what we bring if we don't bring it with a willing heart. The offering God can use is given because of desire, not out of obligation. The offering God can use must be a reflection of what you think about God. If God has been only marginal in your life, you can bring a marginal offering. If God has been only of partial importance in your life, you can bring a partial offering. If God has been a "some-timey" God, you have the liberty to bring a "some-timey" offering. If God has been stingy with you, you can afford to be stingy with God.

But if God has made a way for you, if God has been your bridge over troubled water, if God has been your company-keeper, if God has been your friend when you didn't have a friend, if God has been your lawyer when no one else would come to your defense, if God has been the doctor who has brought your medicine to your room, maybe you ought to bring your offering with a willing heart!

You ought to be glad to bring your offering. As good as God has been to you, nobody should ever have to beg you to bring an offering. As many times as God has lifted you from your bed of affliction, whether to bring a willing offering ought not be a question that you raise. As many tight places as God has brought you out of, as much mess as God has snatched you out of, every chance you get you ought to be running down the aisle to bring your offering.

Notice something else in this text about how the people of Israel were able to build the tabernacle. Not only did they bring their offerings willingly, but they also brought them consistently. Exodus 36:3 says: "And they received of Moses all the offering, which the children of Israel had brought for the work of the service of the sanctuary, to make it withal. And they brought yet unto him free offerings every morning."

This is a word some of you did not want to hear. Some of you live by the principle, "If I give it to you once, don't ask me again!" Some of you say, "I get so sick and tired of going to church when all they talk about is money. I gave them what I'm going to give them, and I ain't going to give them any more. I don't care where they're going or what they're building; if I give them five dollars this year, I don't want them to ask me again next year."

That attitude is not biblical. The text says that the Israelites not only gave with a willing heart, but they gave offerings every morning. Eugene Peterson translates this verse, "The people kept on bringing in their freewill offerings, morning after morning" (MESSAGE). The biblical principle is one of consistency. Since God keeps on sending mornings consistently, I'll keep on bringing my offerings consistently. Since God keeps on putting activity in my limbs every morning, I'll keep on bringing my offerings every morning. Since God keeps on putting the blush in the rose, the clouds in the sky, and the rainbow after the rain, I'll keep on bringing my offerings every morning. Since God keeps on blessing me every morning, I'll keep on bringing my offerings every morning. Since God keeps on letting me drink His water, breathe His air, and eat from His table every morning, I'll keep on bringing my offerings every morning. Since God keeps on anointing my head with oil and preparing a table before me and letting my cup run over every morning, I'll keep on bringing my offerings morning after morning after morning after morning.

How and Who

The strategy that these wilderness people used to accomplish their awesome task was a willing heart and consistent giving. Simply knowing the strategy for building the sanctuary is only one part of the equation, however. We need to know the reasoning as well. So let's look at the reasons the sanctuary was built.

First, the sanctuary was built because the people of Israel learned how to distinguish the *how* from the *who*. Here's what that means. Whenever God places a vision before us that we don't understand, the first question we tend to ask is "*How* can we do this?" And that was the first question Israel asked. Here we are in the wilderness, in a bad location during impossible economic times. How can we do this? We are just like Israel. The task seems larger than we can fathom, the cost represents a burden we think we cannot bear, and no reasonable strategy appears to be in place. *How* can we do this?

We must be careful about asking how. Noah didn't know *how* to float a boat. Moses didn't know *how* to get across the Red Sea. David didn't know *how* to defeat Goliath. The newlyweds didn't know *how* to turn water into wine. Peter didn't know *how* to walk on water. The disciples didn't know *how* to feed five thousand people. Be careful about asking how, for whenever you ask the question, you are relying on human knowledge, which is never sufficient for the moment. Whenever you ask the question "How?" you are implying that for you to achieve a task it needs to make sense to you. That's why Israel later discovered that the question they needed to ask was not "How?" but "Who?"

Who can build a boat in a desert and then order up the rain? God can. *Who* can open up the Red Sea? God can. *Who* can kill Goliath with one stone? God can. *Who* can turn water into wine? God can. *Who* can feed five thousand with two little fish and five loaves of bread? God can. Who can teach you how to walk on water? God can. *Who* can open up a drugstore in the hem of His garment? God can. And *who* can build sanctuaries in the wilderness? God can. The question we need to ask is not "How?" but "Who?"

The second reason the Israelites built the sanctuary was because they remembered where they had come from. They remembered long days spent making bricks without straw under the watchful eyes of Pharaoh's slave masters. They knew that the Lord had brought them a mighty long way.

Some of us here can remember where we came from. We know that nobody but the Lord has brought us from where we used to be to where we are now. Somebody can say, "The Lord brought me ..."; "The Lord taught me ..."; "The Lord kept me ..."; "The Lord never left me. ..." I don't know about you, but I can't forget what He has done for me. I can't forget how He set me free. I can't forget how He brought me out. I don't know about you, but the Lord didn't just bring me a mighty long way; He brought me *all* the way.

There is a third reason the people of Israel built the sanctuary: They built it because they knew they were going somewhere. No matter how attached you are to your present location, God has a better place. I don't mind building the sanctuary, because I know I'm going to a better place, a place where every day is Sunday and Sabbaths have no end. There is a place where the wicked cease from troubling and weary souls can be at rest. There is a place where I will go if this earthly tent is dissolved. It is a house not made with hands, eternal in the heavens. There is a place where my name is written in the Lamb's Book of Life. I don't know about you, but I'm willing to build this tabernacle, because I won't be here long. I'm going somewhere.

Finally, the people of Israel built the sanctuary because they had come to serve the God of too much stuff! It's here in the text:

> And they spake unto Moses, saying, The people bring much more than enough for the service of the work, which the LORD commanded to make. And Moses gave commandment, and they caused it to be proclaimed throughout the camp, saying, Let neither man nor woman make any more work for the offering of the sanctuary. So the people were restrained from bringing. For the stuff they had was sufficient for all the work to make it, and too much. (Exod. 36:5–7)

This is what happened: The people started bringing their offering for the construction of the tabernacle. They brought what they had, and they brought it with a willing spirit. They brought their offering on Monday and Tuesday. In fact, they brought it every morning of the week. They were serious about giving and serious about doing God's work. They were serious about building the sanctuary. They gave so much that the workmen discovered they had too much stuff. They had so much, in fact, that they had to restrain the people from bringing more offerings.

We serve a God of too much stuff! Whatever you want, God's got it. Whatever you need God's got it. He's got enough, and He's got too much stuff.

"Ask, and it shall be given you; seek, and ye shall find; knock, and it shall be opened unto you" (Matt. 7:7). God's got too much stuff.

There is no good thing that the father will withhold from His children. God's got too much stuff.

"My God shall supply all your need according to his riches in glory by Christ Jesus" (Phil. 4:19). God's got too much stuff.

"Bring ye all the tithes into the storehouse, that there may be meat in mine house, and prove me now herewith, saith the LORD of hosts, if I will not open you the windows of heaven, and pour you out a blessing, that there shall not be room enough to receive it" (Mal. 3:10). God's got too much stuff.

"Honour the LORD with thy substance, and with the firstfruits of all thine increase: so shall thy barns be filled with plenty, and thy presses shall burst out with new wine" (Prov. 3:9–10). God's got too much stuff.

When you think about how blessed you've been, why you have what you have, it is because you serve a God with too much stuff.

The clothes in your closet—too much stuff!

The food in your refrigerator—too much stuff!

The money in your pocket—too much stuff!

The condominium you live in—too much stuff!

Those degrees on your wall—too much stuff!

When you wonder on some sweet day who it was that built this tabernacle, just look at God!

OLD ROOTS TRANSPLANTED WITH ROOM TO GROW

Historic Black D.C. Church Breaks Ground for a New Life in the Suburbs

Nelson Hernandez. *The Washington Post*. Washington, D.C.: Apr 12, 2004. Pg. B.05

April 12, 2004

Richard Smallwood's face was glossy with sweat yesterday as he sang "Every Knee Shall Bow," cheered on by a choir of over a hundred and 3,000 churchgoers in their Sunday best clapping, stamping their feet and praising Jesus.

"Is somebody thankful this morning?" Smallwood thundered into the microphone. "Is somebody grateful this morning? Is somebody gratefully thankful this morning?" The crowd, writhing with spirit, roared its thanks.

And that was how Metropolitan Baptist Church, one of the District's oldest and largest black churches, began its move to the suburbs. With an Easter celebration that could wake the dead, the churchgoers—gathered in a giant tent—broke ground on their new 37-acre campus in Largo near Prince George's Community College, reaching the final phase of their 139-year stay at 12th and R streets NW in the Cardozo-Shaw neighborhood and acknowledging the transformation in their congregation.

The sprawling church, started in 1864 by 10 freed slaves worshiping in a Civil War barracks, has more than 6,000 members and 60 ministries, from the Cherub Choir to the Marriage Enrichment Ministry to the Prison Ministry, and five subsidiary corporations including a day school.

But the church's ties to the District have weakened slowly as most of its members have moved to the suburbs. Half the congregation lives in Prince George's County, and another sizable portion lives in Virginia. The influx of the suburbanites, who flood parking spaces each Sunday in a neighborhood in which most of them no longer live, has caused friction over the years with the up-and-coming—and increasingly white—Shaw neighborhood.

Metropolitan's pastor, the Rev. H. Beecher Hicks Jr., said the move was necessary to give the church room to keep growing. The future church, a modern-looking structure shaped somewhat like an M, will have an increased number of classrooms, a "floating" chapel with glass walls and 1,500 parking spaces. It should be completed in a year and a half, church officials said.

"We have a need to be able to expand our ministry ... in order to address the needs of our community," Hicks said in an interview before the ceremony. "We believe this land was given to us providentially.... It was almost as if this land was lying fallow, waiting for us."

The Prince George's County government has been waiting for Metropolitan Baptist, too. "We're delighted to have you here in Prince George's County, because half of you are residents already," said Derrick Green, County Executive Jack B. Johnson's deputy chief of staff, in remarks to the congregation yesterday.

Green went on a religious riff himself as he explained how he hoped the church could combat problems with crime and poverty. "We have many Goliaths that we need to strike down," he said.

The church's current site was sold in December 2002 to Unity of Washington Church, said Denise Gibson-Bailey, Metropolitan's chief operating officer.

Yesterday's chilly, rainy weather did not dampen the enthusiasm inside the tent. "I've been worried all week," Hicks said about the weather forecast. But then he remembered that it also rained on the day he became pastor, on June 17, 1977. "When the rain comes, God's getting ready to do something," he said.

In his homily, after reading the story of Moses and the burning bush from the Bible, Hicks, speaking in the deep, rolling cadences of a master preacher, likened the church's move to the enslaved Israelites' journey from a familiar place into the desert.

"We stand today on sacred soil," he said. "This is not holy ground just because you showed up.... But if this is the ground that God walks upon, if this is the secret place of the Almighty, then this indeed is holy ground."

Staff writer Caryle Murphy contributed to this report.

AN INCREDIBLE ASSIGNMENT IN AN UNLIKELY PLACE

Resurrection and Groundbreaking Sunday 2004
Exodus 3:4–5

And when the LORD saw that he turned aside to see, God called unto him out of the midst of the bush, and said, Moses, Moses. And he said, Here am I. And he said, Draw not nigh hither: put off thy shoes from off thy feet, for the place whereon thou standest is holy ground. (Exod. 3:4–5)

I have a story to tell. It is the story of a people upon whom the hand of God had come to rest. It is a story of a God-man encounter somewhere in the sheep fields of Midian around about Mount Sinai. Biblical scholars tell us it is the story of theophany, that special moment when time and space intersect, when the Eternal is made manifest to mortal man. It is the story of a stuttering and stammering shepherd, called upon to speak of a vision that even he does not fully comprehend.

I have a story to tell. It is the story of an incredible assignment in an unlikely place. It is not a long story, but it is an old story. It is the story of a people caught in the grip of slavery, who found themselves making brick without straw and mortar without clay. Here, within the worn and tattered pages of this book called Exodus, is a word regarding how God moves and how God acts between the lines of human history.

So here you have it. The children of Israel are enslaved. It is within the purposeful intention of God to set them free, to liberate captives, and to usher them from the land of slavery to the land of freedom, a land they said flowed with milk and with honey.

Who shall lead them to their God-directed destination? God chooses an old man—a man whom everyone knows is eighty years old. God chooses, of all persons, a convict, a fugitive from justice, a former prince of Egypt, one Moses by name.

Nobody knows where Moses came from. He spent the first forty years of his life being a "somebody"; he spent the second forty years of his life being a "nobody." But God chose Moses. Not only does God choose him, but God meets him in a desert place, a forsaken place, a place that he calls "the backside of the desert." He meets Moses there for the purpose of giving instructions on how to get the people from over there to over here. God encounters Moses at a summit on Sinai in order to advise him on how to make the transition from where they have been to where he wants them to be. God speaks directly to Moses and prepares to instruct him on how to relocate refugees, how to expand the place of exiles, how to enlarge his territory, and how to take this desert movement from one place to the next. All God wants is to show Moses how to lead God's people from a land called Goshen to a land filled with promise.

In order for God to meet Moses, He conceals Himself. He hides Himself in the branches of a bush, sets it on fire, but then does not permit the bush to burn itself up.

In the moment that Moses sees what can only be described as a phenomenon of nature, in the moment that Moses sees what cynics and skeptics may call an "optical illusion," in the moment that Moses sees what you and I call a "burning bush," God speaks.

In the fire, from the fire, with the fire, God speaks.

God speaks with clarity, calls Moses by his first name, and then tells him not to take another step and to take off his shoes, for the ground on which he is standing is "holy ground"!

This is the essence of my story. God still acts in human history. God still acts in human history in ways we do not understand. God still has plans to guide God's people to a place of God's own choosing. God holds meetings in strange and peculiar places. God still shows up in bush country. Not only that, when God meets you there, God will be accompanied by fire.

In the fire, from the fire, and with the fire, God speaks.

God speaks with clarity, calls you by your first name, and then tells you not to take another step. Take off your shoes, for the ground on which you are standing is "holy ground"!

Surely, this encounter of God with Moses occasions questions:

Where is this place where God holds impromptu church meetings?

Where is this place where God shows up with an agenda that we did not create and that our structures did not approve?

Where is this place where, without consultation, God expects to make announcements of His intention for expansion and relocation?

Where is this place where God imposes His will and vision upon us without our consent?

A Desert Meeting

If this Book is to be believed, God will meet you in the desert. This is what the Book says—so evidently the desert is where God lives, where God shows up, where God does God's best work.

In the desert.

Isaiah said he found "streams in the desert" (Isa. 35:6). Not only that, but Isaiah said that if you're trying to locate God's whereabouts, you should "make straight in the desert a highway for our God" (40:3). That's the path He most often takes.

Jesus could not begin His ministry until He had an encounter with Satan in the desert. Jesus told His disciples that they would find rest in the desert.

John the Baptist was found baptizing, preaching and teaching in the wilderness of Judea—in other words, he set up church in the desert.

Philip converted an Ethiopian eunuch and found a way to baptize him in water he just happened to find in the desert.

When God met Moses, He met him in a desert . . . on the backside of the desert. He met him in a wasteland, a harsh place, a place of poverty and want. When God met Moses, He met him in a place you don't want to be. Do not discount the fact that God met Moses in the desert.

In point of fact, most likely, when you met God, you met God in your desert.

If you have had an encounter with God, no doubt that encounter occurred on some "backside" of your life.

If you are honest, the truth of the matter is that you met God in some back room, in some back alley, out in the middle of nowhere, in your lonely place, in the place of your pain, in the place of your poverty. You met God in your desert.

If you are honest, you met God yesterday in a place you wouldn't want to be today.

The truth is, whenever and wherever you were converted, you met God in your very own, private, and personal desert.

That's the way God works.

Sometimes God does not address your need until He finds you in the desperation of your desert.

Sometimes God does not reveal God's plans for your life until you are out of your comfort zone.

Sometimes God cannot get your attention until God can move you away from the familiar.

God cannot speak to you as long as you are in the palace of your yesterday, dining at Pharaoh's table. God has a plan, God has purpose, God has intention for your life—but His intention is not fully revealed and released until He finds you in a desert.

And don't you find it strange that when God finds you in a desert place, that's when His instruction is clear: "Put off thy shoes from off thy feet, for the place whereon thou standest is holy ground."

It is an incredible assignment; it is in an unlikely place. But the revelation for this hour is that the burning bush conversation was held in the first place because God was in the process of making an assignment. The underlying implication of this text is that the children of Israel would soon be on a forced march away from Egypt, across the Red Sea, and on to the land that God had promised. In order to get them there, God first showed up in a bush that burned but was not consumed. The burning bush was there to gain the attention of Moses, but the intention of God was simply to give an assignment.

A Liberation Agenda

"Come now therefore, and I will send thee unto Pharaoh, that thou mayest bring forth my people the children of Israel out of Egypt" (3:10).

Do not . . . I say again . . . do not miss the fact that God has a liberation agenda. The only reason there is a meeting in the desert in the first place is that God has a liberation agenda. God's people were in bondage in Egypt then, and whether you know it or not, Pharaoh may have changed his clothes and his address but God's people are in new forms of bondage even now.

When unemployment is high and you can't find a job, that's bondage.

When the government is willing to spend more money to feed you in jail than it will to teach you at Howard University, that's bondage.

When our schools pass out diplomas that your children cannot read, that's bondage.

When the nation is captivated by a president who sends young men and women off to find weapons that are not there and then sends a black woman to sit in a hot seat that should be reserved for him, that's bondage.

And that's why God has Moses out there in the first place—because God has a liberation agenda. God wants to set somebody free. Right here on this ground God wants to set somebody free.

Free from bondage.

Free from pain.

Free from trials.

Free from tribulation.

Free from sickness.

Free from poverty.

Free from low self-esteem.

Free from tears.

The only reason we have for being out in this desert even now is that God has a liberation agenda.

Proclamation and Location

Come closer and look to this Word. The only reason God met Moses at his burning bush was that God intended for Moses to say something. It was important for God to hold a meeting in the desert, in the middle of a bush, in the presence of fire, because God had an assignment for Moses to say something.

Maybe what is important here is not location, but proclamation. When God decides to pick you up from where you are over there and set you down over here, the important value is not where you are situated, but what you do after you get there.

Moses, you're over there, but I want you to go over here. I want you to go over here because that's where I want you to say something.

Moses, it's not about your address. I know you've lived at this desert address for forty years.

Moses, tell the children of Israel it's not about their address. I know they've lived where they've lived for four hundred years.

Moses, tell Metropolitan it's not about their address. I know the record; I know they've been there for a hundred and forty years.

It's not about location; it's about proclamation.

The reason I'm moving you from over there to over here is that I want you to say something.

Somebody over here needs to know who I am.

Somebody over here needs to know that I am an intergenerational God—the God of Abraham, Isaac, and Jacob.

Somebody over here needs to hear a prophetic word—a word aptly spoken to those who sit in seats of power and authority.

Somebody over here needs to hear a preached word—a word preached in season and out of season.

Somebody over here needs to know that I am a delivering God.

Somebody over here needs to know that I am a liberating God.

Somebody over here needs to know that I am still in the business of setting captives free.

This is serious business. This is not about location; it's about proclamation. And, by the way, "Put off thy shoes from off thy feet, for the place whereon thou standest is holy ground."

I have a story to tell. And this story is rather simple in its telling. God encounters Moses in his desert. There is a conversation. The conversation, however, is not about location; it is about proclamation. The conversation occurs in the midst of a bush that is on fire but is not consumed. And the end of the conversation is that Moses must take off his shoes, for he is standing on holy ground.

And that's where I'm caught. I am caught trying to make sense out of this burning bush/barefoot/holy ground situation. Let's work it through.

Fire and Risk

The revelation here is that the fire represents risk. The principle is that you cannot be involved in a work for God that does not involve risk. What God calls upon Moses to proclaim—and what

God, through Moses, will require the people to achieve—necessarily involves risk. For Moses, the reality was that in the process of expansion and relocation he would find himself in the fire.

Evidently, when God sets you apart, He also sets you up. This assignment involves risk. If you say you're going to speak for God, there is a significant element of risk. If you stand before the people of God to declare the Word of God and that word involves a disturbance of the status quo, when that word involves change, when that word involves doing things in ways that we've never seen before, this swiftly becomes a matter of major risk.

The risk is that someone will misunderstand.

The risk is that someone will misinterpret your motive as a matter of ego rather than a matter of Spirit.

The risk is that in your desert you will be deserted. Those upon whom you had relied will walk away, subject you to ridicule and scorn, scandalize your name, deny the authenticity of the vision, and call you a fool.

The risk is that you will be caught in an unnatural environment of suspicion and distrust, where the very imperative of God is called into question.

The risk is that not only will there be a fire but that you will be caught up in the fire.

But that's why I am here, why we are here, because we serve a God of risk.

The God I serve is able to float Noah and his ark through a flood, but Noah had to take a risk.

The God I serve is able to handle Goliath and his Philistines, but David first had to take a risk.

The God I serve is able to protect from lions in their den, but Daniel had to take a risk.

The God I serve is able to shield from a burning, fiery furnace, but those three Hebrew boys first had to take a risk.

Peter had within him the power to walk on water, but he had to be willing to take a risk.

Jesus had redemption in His head, salvation in His heart, and grace in His hand, but one Good Friday, at a place called Calvary, even Jesus had to take a risk.

Moses was on his way to the danger of drowning in the Red Sea, but the fire on Sinai was there to remind him that in order to make it over from where he was to where God wanted him to be, he had to be ready to take a risk.

So, then, if we serve a God of risk . . .

Don't tell me what cannot be done: "All things work together for good" (Rom. 8:28)!

Don't tell me what we do not have: "My God shall supply all your needs according to his riches in glory" (Phil. 4:19).

Don't tell me about your fears: "If ye have faith as a grain of mustard seed, ye shall say unto this mountain, Remove hence to yonder place, and it shall remove" (Matt. 18:20).

Don't tell me about enemies and foes: "The LORD shall cause thine enemies that rise up against thee to be smitten before thy face: they shall come out against thee one way, and flee before thee seven ways" (Deut. 28:7).

Don't tell me how impossible this is. Nehemiah said the people built the wall because they had a mind to work.

Don't tell me how hard it is. Isaac had to redig old wells in the middle of a famine, but the Bible says that "Isaac sowed in that land, and received in the same year an hundredfold: and the LORD blessed him" (Gen. 26:12).

And by the way, don't let me forget to tell you. Don't come any closer. Don't go another step farther. Take the shoes from off your feet, for the ground on which you are standing is holy ground!

The Risk God Takes

Look at that burning bush. That bush not only represents the risk we take, but also the risk God takes! The revelation here is patent. Whatever God intends to achieve on this ground, God is counting on us to do it. Listen! God is taking a risk with us.

"What do you mean, preacher? How does God take a risk?" You don't understand. The reason we're here right now is that one day God took a risk.

God took a risk by being born into this world.

God took the risk to be ridiculed and ostracized.

God took the risk to be despised and rejected.

God took the risk to be crucified at the hands of sinful men.

God took the risk to become sin who knew no sin.

God took the risk to die on Calvary's tree.

God took the risk to be buried in Joseph's brand new tomb.

God took the risk to preach to the spirits in hell.

God took the risk to sleep all night Friday, all night Saturday—and then He got up on Sunday morning with all power in His hand.

God took a risk!

God in the Bush

Let me repeat the text one more time:

> And the angel of the LORD appeared unto him in a flame of fire out of the midst of a bush . . . God called unto him out of the midst of the bush. (Exod. 3:2, 4)

Here's the revelation: God does not place you at risk, confine you to a bush, leave you in a desert, take you to a mountain, set you on fire, and then walk away. God does not permit you to absorb all the risk and take no part in it. God spoke to Moses out of the bush. God spoke to Moses out of the flaming fire. The operative reality here is not the bush, but the voice that is in the bush.

Here's the revelation: Before Moses got to the bush, God was already in it. By the time Moses got to the fire, God was already waiting for him.

God's intentions are clear. God intends to liberate God's people. God intends for Moses to be a spokesman on His behalf. God is more interested in proclamation than He is in location. God has a place—another place where God intends for His people to dwell. But in order to get them there, God must take the risk of His own involvement in and commitment to the process. God must take the risk of dealing with us.

First of all, God had to take the risk of dealing with Moses. Moses, by all accounts, was a murderer, a convict, an exile. He was an incognito slave who had been "passing" for something he was not. He stuttered when he talked; he lacked communication skills. And for forty years he had been assigned to the unenviable task of presiding over stinking sheep on the backside of a desert. God took a risk with Moses!

But in addition to that, God takes a risk with *us.*

Us . . . of the unreliable, undependable crew.

Us . . . of the "sometimey," wishy-washy set.

Us . . . of the "I won't give until I see it coming out of the ground" group.

Us . . . of the skeptical "I don't see the vision" crowd.

Us . . . who walk by sight and not by faith!

Us . . . who shout on Sunday but forget Him on Monday.

Please hear me! God is counting on us. God has taken a risk with us. This is no minor moment; this is a serious engagement, and God is counting on us. The integrity of God is caught up in this assignment. God has signed His name to the contract. The signature of God will sign the note. God is counting on us.

He could have chosen someone else—but He chose us.

Maybe He should have chosen someone else—but He chose us.

He could have placed this ground in some other hands—but He chose us.

He could have invested His resources in some other people—but He chose us.

God has taken a risk with us. And that's the reason you need to take off your shoes, for the ground on which you are standing is holy ground!

Did I tell you this is holy ground? But it is not holy ground just by calling it that.

This is not holy ground just because you showed up.

This is not holy ground just because you've brought an offering and you think you've done enough.

This is holy ground when you realize that it took a struggle just to get you here.

All I'm trying to get you to understand is that we are not here by accident. We are not here by chance, by circumstance, or by luck. We are here because God has been working for 140 years just to get us to this place.

It took a lot of praying just to get this far.

It took a lot of preaching just to get this far.

The adversaries have been many. The road has not been easy. The path has not been straight. The plow with tears is wet. And yet we are here by God's mercy. We are here by God's goodness. We are here by God's grace, and that makes this ground holy ground!

This is holy ground whenever you realize that God has taken the ordinary and set it aside for a holy purpose! And doesn't it dawn on you that God tends to use ordinary dirt for extraordinary purposes?

In the morning of creation God stooped down to the dust of the earth, scooped up a handful of dirt, molded it in His own image, and then blew into it the breath of life. Just ordinary dirt.

One day Jesus ran into a blind man, picked up a little dirt in his hand, mixed it with a little spit, and told him to go wash in the pool of Siloam. And the Bible says he came forth seeing, but all Jesus used for the surgery was some ordinary dirt.

I looked further and discovered that Jesus came upon a woman—they say she was caught in the very act of adultery. He didn't say anything. He just got down on His knees and started writing. "Woman, where are your accusers? All I have here is some ordinary dirt."

It's just ordinary dirt. This is just ground. It is only ground . . . soil . . . sand . . . dirt . . . trees . . . bushes. It's just dirt.

This is not a place for the Colosseum at Rome.

This is not a site to rival the Taj Mahal.

The Great Wall of China would never fit on this terrain.

This would never be a place chosen for awe and splendor and wonder.

By the valuations of men no one would ever proclaim this land as valuable. It's just dirt.

But if this is the ground that God walks on,

—If this is the ground God walks in the cool of the evening,

—If this is the ground where God chooses to make His tabernacle,

—If this is the place where God decides to dwell,

—If this is the place where a soul can meet a Savior,

—If this is the secret place of the Most High,

—If this is the place where you can stand under the shadow of the Almighty,

—If this is the place where God shows up from time to time,

This is holy ground.

We have an incredible assignment in an unlikely place. It's just dirt, but it's holy.

You cannot make it holy.

You cannot proclaim it holy.

You cannot put a sign on it and declare that it is holy.

The only way in which the ground becomes holy is when you discover that every time you come to this place you are standing in the presence of God.

You will not stand in the presence of men. That will not make it holy.

You will not stand in the presence of those who claim the pretensions of earthly power. That will not make it holy.

You will not stand in the presence of angels, for even the singing of angels will not make it holy.

Even if 144,000 should come to join us, that still will not make it holy.

Only when you stand in His presence—

Only when you stand in the presence of the Alpha and the Omega—

Only when you stand in the presence of the great I AM—

Only when you stand in the presence of the One who has named you and claimed you—

Only when you stand in the presence of the One who has been your help in ages past and will be your hope for years to come—

Only when you stand in the presence of the One who is the lovely chief of all your joy—

Only then are you standing on holy ground.

> *Holy, holy, holy, Lord God Almighty!*
> *Early in the morning our song shall rise to Thee.*
> *Holy, holy, holy, merciful and mighty!*
> *God in three persons, blessed Trinity!*

The word for this hour is "take off your shoes, for the ground on which you are standing is holy ground!"

Do You See What I See?

The matter of vision is complex when the pastor discovers that what he or she sees is entirely different from what the people see. The inescapable and relentless task of the watchperson-priest is to labor with worn-out tools until those who hear are also able to see. Therefore vision must not only be cast, but also taught repeatedly. A vision once spoken is twice forgotten, but a vision that is spoken with regularity and precision—and, as with Moses, dramatically—makes its way to the head and subsequently to the heart.

ON JORDAN'S
STORMY BANKS

I suspect that in God's mind the preacher never preaches multiple sermons, only one. Throughout the whole of ministry, the priest-watchperson climbs the tower week after week to declare a new word, a new vision, a new thing that God is doing or requiring. Every sermon, however, ends with a comma or a semicolon, never with a period. There is always more to come—new insights, new vision—intended to be shared.

Those of us who are engaged in this preaching profession preach with the hope that not only will we cast a vision, but that in doing so our own vision will be sharpened. Our goal is not only to instruct, but also to be instructed through the process. We seek not only to speak a word to the people on behalf of God, but also to hear God speaking to us directly and personally.

Vision casting is an imprecise art, a process of trial and error, a continuous and relentless process that goes through phases of discovery and change. The phases of vision casting are both sequential and concurrent, but they always reflect a process of becoming, never a state of being.

In sum, this book is designed to share what I have learned in the hope that others will benefit. What insights have I gained?

1. Proper Planning Is Essential to Effective Visioning and Vision Implementation.

It is critical that the watchperson-priest have help from persons who are able to give critical thought to the task at hand and to the outcomes that are expected. The larger the group of persons for whom one is casting vision, the more important is intentional planning of the step-by-step vision-casting process. No matter how insightful or visionary the priest-watchperson, he or she cannot think of everything and cannot achieve his or her purposes alone. Authentic leadership never stands alone. The leader's task is never fulfilled in isolation. One who leads with integrity clearly understands that no one can ever do it all, because no one really knows it all. Our pews are filled with talented, Spirit-filled laypersons who can help broaden and deepen the scope of our vision. We must permit a collaborative process that allows them to do so. We all need help, so ask for it, use it, and benefit from it.

2. Keep the People Informed.

It is of vital importance that the congregation be kept abreast of the elements of the vision, the progress that is being made, and the manner in which the life of the church, collectively and individually, is being changed by it. The New Birth Baptist Church of Miami, Florida, is an example of creative vision-sharing. During the time their church was under construction, a video of the work in progress was presented in each Sunday service. From week to week the congregation could see the foundation being poured, the sides and roof going up, the plumbing and electrical work being completed, the carpet being laid, and the furnishings being set in place. This kind of information sharing permitted the congregation to be involved, to be a part of the process, and to know that their offerings were being put to good use. The vision literally was kept before the people's eyes. When we keep the vision before the congregation's eyes, it will become embedded in their hearts.

3. The Pastor Is Central to the Vision-Casting and Buy-In Process.

The pivotal thesis of this book is that preaching is vital to the vision-casting process. Yet we must be cautious about what we preach. Sermons should concentrate on spiritual matters rather than exclusively on physical matters. If all people hear from the pulpit is "building," they will never hear ministry, which is the far more critical issue.

The priest-watchperson must remember that the last thing those in the pews want to hear sermonically is something to do with a building or with money. Every vision cast before the church must be couched in ministry terms, or it will suffer the criticism that the vision is self-serving, that the pastor is engaged in personal "kingdom building," and that the church is avoiding more critical issues that confront it.

As I reflect on my casting of the vision for Metropolitan Baptist Church, I realize that the first mistake I made was to create an organizational structure for the achievement of the vision before we ensured the congregation's spiritual buy-in. A far better process would have been to cast the vision with small groups of people, beginning with key leaders, then casting a wider and wider net until larger and larger segments of the congregation were included, informed, and involved.

4. The Congregation Sees the Person Before They See the Vision.

We would like to believe that the vision and the visionary are separate. In reality, however, they are often perceived as one in the same. For example, Bill Gates personifies the vision for Microsoft; and Jack Welch was completely identified with General Electric's vision, its fortunes, and its failings. Similarly, the congregation will tend (as my own certainly did and does) to see the vision as synonymous with the visionary. Who we are and who we are perceived to be may get in the way of the vision's acceptance. The question for the congregation is not what is being proposed but who is making the proposition.

When casting a vision, the visionary's perceived level of integrity is a primary concern. In fact, the watchperson and the very integrity of God both are at stake. As watchmen we are not expected to be perfect. None of us is perfect. Thus, God chooses watchpersons not because we are perfect, but because we are available. At the same time, how we carry ourselves as watchpersons influences the amount of credibility we have and the trust we receive. The congregation wants to sense that we are believable and sincere and that our vision is authentic. They want to sense that the trust they invest in terms of their time, energy, and finances is well spent.

Credibility and trust are not developed overnight. They are the result of months and years of interaction. Every watchperson on the wall is not trusted on his or her first night on duty. They may call you "Pastor," but until you have been through trials and tribulation and have been weighed in the balance and found faithful, you are just another preacher.

5. Competing Voices within the Church Make It Difficult for the Congregation to Hear What Is Truly Being Said.

While the watchperson-priest may be the only visionary who is acknowledged within the congregation, he or she certainly is not the only voice that is heard. Many people within our congregations have ideas that are far different from the vision we are seeking to cast, and they are not shy about expressing their views. The Internet has created the ability of persons in our pews to share their opinions swiftly with large numbers of people with the simple press of a computer key.

Why are these other voices heard? They are heard because their experience in other organizations has given them a voice to give shape to their own visions. Their knowledge makes them believe it should easily be transferred to and valued in the church. And they bring their Bibles as well as their leadership experience. Therefore, the day of the pastor as the only recognizable and acceptable voice, if not gone, is certainly diminished.

Whenever this discussion is raised, most of us in the pastoral profession will swiftly retort that God gives the vision to only one person and that the anointing goes first to the head and then flows down. Many sermons emphasize the fact that the anointing is not applied to elbows and kneecaps. God does not expect the feet and hands to do what the head is designed to do. I'll say "Amen" to that!

However, if we are to be the visionaries, if we are to be the authentic voice of God among the people, then we had better be prepared to demonstrate it and prove it. The persons who fill the pews of our churches don't just want to passively hear of the vision; they want to approve of it. Church members are hard-pressed to entrust the life of the community to the notions of one person even if that person is the one they designated as leader-pastor.

In every church somebody other than the pastor is talking, and many persons are listening to those voices. It is important for the pastor to listen as well.

One other word regarding the role of the pastor-visionary within the church is critical here. God did not need Moses to get Israel into the Promised Land. God could take care of that business himself. Moses was the instrument to take God's people from where they were to where God wanted them to be—nothing more, nothing less. This is a sobering but necessary thought for every watch-person who stands in the tower of visionary leadership.

6. No Matter How Precise Your Language, It Will Be Difficult for the Congregation to Conceptualize the Vision.

For most persons, visions are difficult to define and therefore difficult to grasp. Visions are believed to stem from imagination; they are flights of fancy. Visions are hard to accept because they often seem divorced from reality, floating in the realm of the unachievable and unattainable. Visions are accomplished only through faith, a commodity most of us have in short supply. Visions are almost always expensive, and most of us do not have the blessing of an inexhaustible money tree. Therefore, when the priest-watchperson speaks of visions, he or she faces immediate suspicion simply because the people cannot believe it or see it, do not wish to pay for it, and often will not pray for it.

It is critical that the priest-watchperson be certain of the direction the vision is leading. In most instances, as was the case with Moses, those who were following him could not see where he was going. Not only are members of our congregations unable to see the vision, those to whom we speak of the vision will filter our words through the lenses of their personal, often selfish, needs and desires. Buy-in for the vision must come from those whose primary interest is in what the vision can do for them and how it will change the quality of their lives spiritually, psychologically, and physically. The vision must promise a blessing that is both individual and collective.

The language of the visionary is typically so far afield and far-fetched from reality that it is blurred in the haze of the incredible. The task of the visionary, in simplest terms, is to demonstrate to our followers that the visions of which we speak and preach are not pipe dreams or nocturnal illusions. The task is to remind followers that the vision is secure if for no other reason than that God's name is at stake, God's integrity is on the line, in the process. We must be certain of our destination. And remember that God instructed the prophet Habakkuk to write the vision so a person running could read it. In other words, the task of the visionary is to make the vision larger than life so that even one who is focused on something else can see it and understand it at a glance. Habakkuk's challenge is our challenge. We must do no less.

7. *The Casting of Vision Implies Customized Change.*

Most priests-watchpersons are brought into a particular church setting by the excitement and exuberance of the pulpit committee. In my experience, the pulpit committee is quick to tell the candidate that the church is ready for change. They are certain that the person before them is the right person to bring about that change and take the church to heights that have only been dreamed of. If you ever hear such, don't believe it.

No matter what we are told, the last thing churches want is change. Churches with long histories and traditions are particularly loathe to accept change, because it disrupts their lives and removes them from their comfort zones. The vast majority of churches in American have less than two hundred members because they are places of comfort, not growth.

Consequently, when a vision is cast, the priest-watchperson is challenging "what is" to move to "not yet." In between those two realities lies a tension that can be both threatening and destructive. In my case, I am engaged in a process not only of changing the church, but also of relocating it. The church is 140 years old. The task of moving a historic congregation and challenging its right to remain in its place of comfort for the second time in this ministry is daunting indeed.

It is important, therefore, that vision casting is tailored to fit the needs of a particular congregation. It is critical that the priest-watchperson conduct an internal audit of the ministry in order to understand who is really in leadership, who the stakeholders are, what the role of the community is in shaping the church, and numerous other questions that must be answered before a vision can be presented for the congregation's acceptance.

In addition, whichever strategy for casting the vision is employed must be continually updated. Seasons change; churches change. Old members leave; new members come. Preachers change; you will change. What works today may need to be revised tomorrow. Every church is different. What works in the Metropolitan Church may not work in yours. What fails in the Metropolitan Church may be just the strategy needed in your own. There is no one-size-fits-all vision-casting strategy. Measure the church spiritually, emotionally, and economically, and then be sure that the visionary garment you are producing—consistent with the word and vision God has given you—is well tailored for the people you serve.

8. The Visionary Must Avoid Distractions.

While preaching about the tabernacle and the experience of Moses and the children of Israel, I was given a sure revelation regarding the necessity of protecting the leader. When Moses was leading, over and over again the people murmured and complained. They asked, "Who chose Moses to lead, anyhow? We would have been better off to die back in Egypt."

But Moses would not be distracted. Aaron got bored with the process. He understood the psychology of the masses. He could see that the people didn't want liberation; they wanted to party. They did not want freedom; they wanted foolishness. That's when Aaron and his cohorts designed another campaign and made a golden calf the centerpiece of their effort. They held a planning meeting when they should have been holding a prayer meeting. They put gold where God should have been. And when Moses recorded the event he said, "The people sat down to eat and to drink, and rose up to play" (Exod. 32:6).

The watchperson-priest must always avoid distraction. Distraction is Satan's tool; he tries to get you to take your eyes off what God wants in order to satisfy what the people want. Ther are, of course, legitimate voices of dissent that must be heard. But distraction is Satan's way of establishing the agenda of leadership under the guise of giving good advice and reminding us of the value of "informed consent." Distraction attempts to alter one's course by presenting alternatives. Yet God always deals with a vision. Whenever there is more than one vision, there is always *di-vision*! In every effort, there are those who believe they know more than God knows. They call to provide the pastor with instructions that God failed to share with him or her. Do not be deceived by such thinking. The lesson of Moses' leadership is to avoid distractions at all costs.

9. Vision Casting Takes Time.

No matter how necessary, clear, and compelling your vision may be, a significant period of time must pass before understanding, acceptance, and buy-in occurs. I remain clear that God placed Metropolitan Church at a particular place in history that would demand a strategic shift in its capacity to serve and that sooner or later a physical move would have to take place. That's a hard vision to sell.

We began the vision-casting process with our Vision2000 program in May 1992. At this writing, we have been at this visioning process for over a decade and we still have more years to come. Our experience, however, is not novel. The reason we are always in search of the tabernacle and always in search of Shekinah glory is that the Bible says God sent Moses out on a little journey that should have taken a few days and then stretched it out into forty years!

It is clear that the priest-watchperson must learn the lesson of patience, because whatever your vision is, it will not be achieved without opposition, and it most likely will not be achieved without the expenditure of large quantities of time and money.

10. The Congregation Has a Responsibility.

Thus far we have concentrated solely on the responsibility of the priest-watchperson in his or her role as vision caster. Those in the pews must be given a corresponding responsibility, with accountability. Whatever becomes of the church institutionally is the sole responsibility of the person in the primary leadership role. The congregation must ever be encouraged to remain open to receive the vision God has given. Subsequently, they must act in faith even and especially in times of misunderstanding and conflict.

An atmosphere that encourages the congregation to express honestly their feelings and engage in dialogue must exist so that mutual respect will abound throughout the church. Such honesty, however, must not be permitted to bring about division. God is not the author of confusion. Therefore, there must be a godly resistance that holds high the banner of Christ and rebukes those who, with satanic intent, come against the church, its vision, and its leaders. King David quoted God's words on this issue: "Touch not mine anointed, and do my prophets no harm" (1 Chron. 16:22).

The church must be encouraged to create an environment of wholesome prayer in which acceptance, forgiveness, and love can grow. It is only in such an environment that the vision that God intends for the church can be nurtured for the benefit of the entire community.

Do not misunderstand my intent. I am not insisting that the church must follow the priest-watchperson with blind allegiance. Everyone within the body of Christ must be held to a holy accountability. Nevertheless, once a decision has been made by the congregation to follow visionary leadership, loyalty to that vision and to that leader are essential to the healthy life and future of the church.

Without needless second-guessing and quarrelsome spirits, those in the pew must come to trust leadership to make appropriate decisions. The church must remain in constant prayer for the pastor upon whose shoulders rest an awesome weight of responsibility and sacred charge.

The final responsibility of those in the pews is for lay leadership to aggressively engage in activities and policies that welcome change and innovation for the good of the whole.

11. "Everybody Talkin' 'bout Heaven Ain't Goin' There!"

As with every struggle for institutional change, there will always be tragic losses along the way. If the account of the migration of the children of Israel from Egypt to the Promised Land is instructional at all, it teaches that those who begin the journey do not always complete it. Even Moses, the venerated leader in search of freedom, found that his feet would not touch that sacred soil.

The contemporary church scene is much the same. There are those within the church community who will make a conscious decision not to make the journey because their attachment to the present reality is too great to make the separation. There are those who, because of the exigencies of time and age, are prevented from completing the course. Even the priest-watchperson must approach his or her task with the full knowledge that he or she may not be able to see the eventual end.

In the likely event that there are those who refuse to make the journey, the shepherd must reach out to include them and do what he or she can to encourage them to come along. It is not always possible to do that work of reclamation, however, so the shepherd may painfully have to acknowledge that not everyone will make the journey. This may be a good thing, however, because sometimes there are harmful personalities and bad attitudes that should not be dragged from the old tabernacle to the new! The old gospel hymn "I Am Bound for the Promised Land" raises the question "Oh, who will come and go with me?" because it is true that some will make a conscious decision not to travel. That is also why it is necessary to be assured that the vision is God-given. Scripture warns, "Woe be unto the pastors that destroy and scatter the sheep of my pasture! saith the LORD" (Jer. 23:1).

12. *The Struggle Will Continue.*

Finally, as the church continues through change and growth, its transitional phases do not come to an end, but continue from one stage to the next. Churches will continually face change; congregations will continually resist change. Priests-watchpersons will continue to mount their towers to declare a God-given vision. Those who hear in some distant valley will deny that the message was ever given or that there was some failing on the part of the watchperson to give an authentic word. Everyone who hears the vision will not be convinced of its necessity. Those who are closest to the watchperson will find fault with and blame him or her if the vision is not fulfilled in the way it had been promised or they had expected. The task for the watchperson, however, is not only to be heard, it is to be faithful to the telling and to assure them that God has promised to bring God's people home.

As watchpersons we must be vigilant, on guard, and receptive to the vision God holds for us on tomorrow's horizon. Never give up on the church. Never relinquish the vision. We must never give up on ourselves. We must never give up on God. Remember that while we may fall prey to your personal doubts and fears, the important element in every vision may not be the vision itself but the journey toward it. It is through the journey that the watchperson earns the right to stand at the post. It is through the journey that the people of God learn not only to follow the leader but to trust the God who leads the leader.

We are engaged in a journey toward vision, a journey toward the promised land. The nature of the vision defines the journey and the path we take. The promised land is not a place of the here-and-after; it is a place of the here-and-now. The Promised Land to which Israel journeyed was real. They found more than giants of opposition; they found grapes and pomegranates and figs. The promised land is a real place for real people, and God intends to take God's people to it now. The task of the watchperson-priest is to lead the way. God's task is to safeguard the journey.

We are engaged in a journey toward vision. The task is arduous and merciless. Still, we must never forget that the objective of the journey is larger than the leader. Where we are headed is more important than the one who leads the march. If the vision is authentic, it will always supersede the one to whom it is given. We serve a God who makes provision for the vision, who is with us both in and through the journey, who sustains us on the journey, and who will meet us one day in the land God has promised.

On Jordan's stormy banks I stand and cast a wishful eye;
To Canaan's fair and happy land where my possessions lie.
All o'er those wide extended plains, shines one eternal day;

There God the Son forever reigns and scatters night away.
No chilling winds or pois'nous breath can reach that healthful
shore;

Sickness and sorrow, pain and death are felt and feared no more.
When shall I reach that happy place and be forever blest?

When shall I see my Father's face and in His bosom rest?
I am bound for the Promised Land.

I am bound for the Promised Land.
Oh, who will come and go with me?
I am bound for the Promised Land.

Samuel Stennett

A Personal Word

I have not remained unaffected through all of this. Every day I remain in conversation with God about His direction for my life and ministry. In this book I have taken the risk of being very candid. I have assumed the risk of exposing my inner feelings not only to the congregation I serve but also to the community in which we minister just as I did in *Preaching through a Storm*.[1]

To suggest that I have had no doubts or fears would be disingenuous to the superlative degree. I know the pursuit of this new vision will not be easy. Any victory must come through struggle just as the kingdom of God comes through tribulation. I have reached the point in my life and in my ministry where I am seasoned enough to want to pick my battles. The fact that this desire is, no doubt, an impossibility does not keep me from desiring it. After twenty-seven years in the service of God and Metropolitan, I hope to lead the congregation into a new land and to a new opportunity and paradigm for ministry that does not neglect the rich heritage the church represents as a landmark in the African American community of the District of Columbia.

In that respect, many believe that moving the church is inappropriate and does not at all respect the church's historical significance. Many political, business, and social leaders of the District have offered their opinions about the church's decision and my leadership role in that decision. They have been quick to call attention to the fact that we have a large responsibility to history and must never forsake the contribution of those who have paved the way.

While I agree with their concerns, I have drawn a different conclusion. The church is indeed historic. The value of its history, however, lies not only in what it has already achieved, but also in what it will be able to achieve in the future against the backdrop of its noble foundation. The church is more than a place; it is purpose.

Properly understood, the church is never a static institution; it is ever moving and changing. That which we seek to accomplish in ministry is not tied to a particular location. Rather, it expands in many directions to achieve many purposes. We will still serve the pressing needs of the urban community. God's vision for us includes a continuing social service impact ministry within the District, which includes the Metropolitan Day School (pre-K–8) in northwest Washington. Our primary worship facility will be situated on the new land in Largo, Maryland. The Metropolitan of the future will truly be one church in multiple locations.

This volume cannot come to its close without an acknowledgment of the deep debt of gratitude that I owe to the Metropolitan congregation. These words are the reflections of a leader-pastor-parish priest whose people have given to him the privilege to lead as well as the opportunity to approach daring and innovating methods for ministry. As I have changed, so have we all.

Over these last years we have truly grown together in very special ways. I have no doubt now that while there are those who struggle with the process, it is my hope that we have evolved to a point in our relationship where there is profound respect and love for each other. I was overwhelmed recently when Metropolitan's minister of music, the Reverend Nolan E. Williams Jr., while seated at the piano during worship, penned the words to this song, by which I am humbled and for which I am incredibly grateful:

> *Pastor and people on the word!*
> *Pastor and people under the cross!*
> *Lord, as you've spoken we have heard,*
> *Bind us together, heart in heart.*
> *Bind us together, heart in heart.*[2]

I am convinced that God is at work here. Our task is to get in God's path so that we can be directed toward the place and purpose He has directed and ordained for us. I am a parish priest who is determined to stay on the path wherever it leads.

SELECT BIBLIOGRAPHY

Brown, William. *The Tabernacle: Its Priests and Its Services.* 1872;
   reprinted and revised, Peabody, MA: Hendrickson, 1996.
Higle, Tommy C. *Journey through the Tabernacle.* Marietta, OK:
   Tommy Higle Publishers, n.d.
Moore, Beth. *A Woman's Heart: God's Dwelling Place.* Nashville:
   LifeWay, 1995.
Olford, Stephen F. *The Tabernacle: Camping with God.* Neptune,
   NJ: Loizeaux, 1971.

ENDNOTES

Part 1

1. Quoted in Leonard Sweet, *SoulTsunami* (Grand Rapids: Zondervan, 1999), 45.

Part 3

1. Howard Thurman, *The Centering Moment* (Richmond, IN: Friends United Press, 1969), 52.
2. Terence E. Fretheim, "Exodus," *Interpretation: A Bible Commentary for Teaching and Preaching* (Louisville: John Knox Press, 1991), 1.
3. Biblical instances of the Shekinah can be found in Exodus 24:16; 40:35; Numbers 9:17–18; Revelation 21:22.
4. "Shekinah," *Encyclopedia Judaica*, vol. 14 (Jerusalem: Keter Publishing House, 1972), 1349–51.

A Personal Word

1. H. Beecher Hicks Jr., *Preaching through a Storm* (Grand Rapids: Zondervan, 1987).
2. Nolan E. Williams Jr., NEW-J Publishing, Copyright © 2003.

My Soul's Been Anchored

A Preacher's Heritage in the Faith

H. Beecher Hicks Jr.

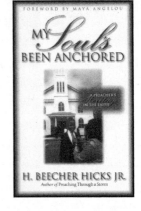

H. Beecher Hicks Jr. knows that great preaching and great storytelling go hand in hand. He believes in the power of imagination to teach us about God and about life, and he knows that nothing can spark the imagination like a story well told. In *My Soul's Been Anchored*, he presents vivid portrayals of the biblical truth shining through people he has known and experiences he has had.

Weaving his life stories around the broad topics of beginnings, the faith, the church, and death and life, Dr. Hicks encourages us to reach for purpose. Put your faith in motion, he urges. Never give up on your potential or God's promises. "I wonder if God wonders," says Dr. Hicks. "I wonder if God dreams. . . . I wonder what the imagination of God must be!" *My Soul's Been Anchored* will help you explore God's imagination and your own. Here is storytelling at it finest from a gifted African-American writer and preacher, with universal truths that speak to every culture. Read, enjoy . . . and grow from the wisdom of these gentle and passionate narratives by H. Beecher Hicks Jr.

Hardcover ISBN: 0-310-22136-6

Pick up a copy today at your favorite bookstore!

Preaching Through a Storm

Confirming the Power of Preaching in the Tempest of Church Conflict

H. Beecher Hicks Jr.

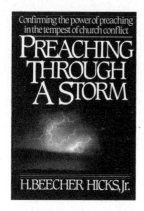

The context was a building program for an urban congregation. The beginning bore no omens of controversy. But before long, both the pastor (the author) and the congregation found themselves in a storm that threatened the church's very existence and the pastor's future in ministry.

It is common in this kind of storm that neither the preacher nor his flock will expect to hear from God. But the arresting message of this book is that it is often through the preaching itself that God speaks to the issues of conflict. It is through preaching that the issues are resolved, and neither the pastor nor the people are left unchanged.

By example and by precept this book shows how to weather a storm in the only successful way—by preaching through it under the guiding hand of a compassionate God who knows our human anguish. This is a book you cannot afford to ignore. For, as one preacher puts it, you're either "coming out of a storm, in a storm, or heading for a storm."

Softcover ISBN: 0-310-20091-1

Pick up a copy today at your favorite bookstore!

ZONDERVAN™

GRAND RAPIDS, MICHIGAN 49530 USA

WWW.ZONDERVAN.COM

We want to hear from you. Please send your comments about this book to us in care of zreview@zondervan.com. Thank you.

GRAND RAPIDS, MICHIGAN 49530 USA

WWW.ZONDERVAN.COM